COURTNEY L. PATTERSON

INSIDE MY
DARKNESS

DARKNESS

MY BLACKER-THAN-ME
SYNDROME

INSIDE MY DARKNESS
My Blacker-than-Me Syndrome

Courtney Patterson
restart2k6@hotmail.com

ISBN 978-1-949826-59-3
Printed in the USA.

Published by: EAGLES GLOBAL BOOKS | Frisco, Texas
In conjunction with the 2023 Eagles Authors Course
Cover & interior designed by DestinedToPublish.com

DEDICATION

I want to dedicate this book to my lovely family who stood with me through all the storms that accompanied the writing of this book. Cynthia, Chris, and Cierra, thank you for believing in me and providing me the space to create. I love you all.

For my mother, Cheryl Patterson, thank you for being the strong black woman who single-handedly and successfully raised three children through challenging times in the neighborhoods of St. Louis, Missouri. Without you, there is no me.

To Solaica: Honestly, you were the fuel to the engine behind the writing of this book. During my downtime and the days that I wanted to quit, you were there to lift me up to continue writing, and your constant prayers kept me rooted. Thank you so much for all you have done to make this a reality. I couldn't have done this without you, and I am forever indebted to you.

ACKNOWLEDGEMENTS

First, I want to give thanks to my Lord and savior, Jesus Christ, for instilling within me the passion, gifting, and wherewithal to pick up a pen and to create a document worthy of Him. I would like to give thanks to my pastor, Dr. E. Christopher Hill, for showing tenacity, resolve, and the courage to teach Kingdom principles to God's people.

I must acknowledge my brothers in arms and faith, Dave Harper, Phil Carter, and Anthony Young, for allowing God to speak and work through you as you all have spiritually poured into my life.

To my VKE family for showing me and the world what a tight and loving family should look like. I want to acknowledge all the friends who chose to walk alongside me through this project.

To Diamond, thank you for bringing levity into my life and causing laughter at times when I couldn't find anything to laugh about. It was true medicine.

ACKNOWLEDGEMENTS

And I want to acknowledge the other dark-skinned blacks who, through it all, made the decision to use that which was placed upon you to serve as a deterrent, as premium rocket fuel in order to propel you to success. This book is to honor you!

To Kara, my coach, Destined to Publish, and EITI for providing the platform and vehicle to help make what was once a thought into a reality.

All the poems contained in this book are original works authored by me.

FOREWORD

A soul syndrome is a complex trap of syncopated circumstances. A perfect storm of soul sickness coming in like a front. A symphony of negative circumstances played by an orchestra from hell.

Many of us have battled these visible and invisible circumstances, but few of us have boldly set our minds and our resolves to first understand our own soul syndromes and then to battle and overcome them.

CP is unquestionably one of the few people who has done just this. And then, he fearlessly and valiantly, with poetic and sometimes pain-filled perception, walks us through his own process in this breakthrough book *Inside My Darkness*.

CP walks us into his past, and with almost poetic prose, he details the very building blocks of the syndrome that sought to permanently entrap his life. He fearlessly, and with great transparency, tells us of the traumas that he experienced while trapped within the confines of those invisible soulical walls.

But he goes on to show us how he bulldozed his way out of those walls, dismantled those bricks, and, with a voraciously victorious spirit, found his own freedom and identity.

This book is not only hopeful and encouraging, but it is powerfully instructive and vitally useful. Because he not only details his syndrome but shows us how to get out of our own.

Your story may not be identical to his in every detail, but his story is so encouraging because he shows us how to both understand our syndromes and break out of them. He does not make us feel like voyeurs—like strangers watching his story unfold before us. He makes us fellow pilgrim travelers on the journey of his walk to freedom.

His insight, his effortless humor, his surgical honesty, and his open humanity laid bare allow us to both laugh and to cry within the span of just a few pages.

This book is not only cathartic but healing, like mental medicine written on pages we can access in the privacy of our own thoughts. He goes public so we can be healed in private. And for this we owe him a great debt.

I know this man personally. So, in reading this work, I can only be overwhelmed by his startling transformation. I can see the man, the hero, the veteran, the husband, and the father that he has become. The wounds of his past battles have not deterred him from his greatest life goals, nor have they diminished his shine. He has conquered the darkness—and has captured the light. He has redefined himself and taught us that we can do the same.

At the onset of this book, CP promises us that his story will affect our lives in several different ways. He says that it will enhance our own self-awareness. And that it will ignite in us a burning desire to seek avenues for our own change. He further promises to give us the tools that will help us make better life decisions and that will enhance our insight into the hidden reasons for the actions of others. But I think the best promise that CP makes to us is that this book will leave us better equipped to identify the triggers of our own syndromes.

After reading this work, I can say without question or doubt that *Inside My Darkness* overdelivers on all of these promises.

This book will entertain you, transport you, and enlighten you, but it will also empower you to heal in areas where you may not have even realized that you were broken.

Dr. Chris Hill

PRESIDENT
HILL COMMUNICATIONS GROUP

ENDORSEMENT

Thank you for sharing your book, your thoughts, and a piece of your life with me. I am truly in awe of your strength and ability to find humor in many difficult moments. I am humbled and honored to know you. Your book is thought-provoking and as inspiring as it is funny! You have given me much to think about, personally. The thing that really makes me think hard is your description of the rocks exercise. You describe it so vividly. It is an example of a compelling narrative AND a life lesson—I am very much working on getting rid of many of my own rocks. I think the thing that I love best is how it is YOUR voice. Reading this, I imagine we are on one of our many hour-long Zoom calls. I enjoy that conversational tone in your writing, and I think other readers will, too.

Lisa C. Brunner

ATTORNEY

TABLE OF CONTENTS

INTRODUCTION

Everyone has some type of syndrome to contend with. Wait! Now I understand that this is a bold statement for someone who doesn't even know you to make, and trust me, before I discovered my own personal syndrome, I would have reacted the exact same way. However, I can offer you this: By the time you finish this book, that statement may not seem that far-fetched. In actuality, you may even agree with me. Before we continue with this book, let's get some basic facts out of the way.

What is a syndrome? According to the experts at genome. gov, a syndrome is "a collection of distinctive features that tend to manifest in groups of individuals with the same disease." Now before you go saying I said you have a disease, let us explore this word *syndrome* a little further. The word syndrome stems from the Greek word σύνδρομον, or *sundrom*, which means occurrence or running together, and when it is paired with a specific and definite cause, it is then that it transitions to a disease.

According to a 2015 article by Dinethra Menon for Health Writer Hub, a syndrome typically refers to a collection of signs or symptoms that characterize or tend to suggest a specific disease. A disease, conversely, results from a pathophysiological response to external or internal factors that cause abnormalities in the systemic functions of the body that may cause physical and emotional pain, as well as dysfunction, distress, social problems, or even death.

Trust me, this book is not going to talk about the morbid end of diseases or even how symptoms can turn into diseases, but I felt that we need to get the boring scientific stuff out of the way to help set a foundation that we can build upon. However, I will warn you ahead of time that I will have to define a couple more terms later that will also assist us along this journey you have chosen to embark upon with me.

With over 2700 categorized syndromes and 6800+ named syndromes, I probably could have said that based on the laws of probability, there is an extreme likelihood that you experience at least one of these syndromes, but what's the fun in doing that? Now please understand I am no doctor and the only background I have in medicine is earning my first aid merit badge in the Boy Scouts. Neither am I a psychologist or psychiatrist, as my educational background is in art history, nuclear physics, mathematics, business management, religious studies, and leadership. Despite my education in all these fields, I am in no way an expert on the psychology of syndromes on the human experience. I am, however, an expert in my own personal syndrome, and by being transparent, I feel that I can help you identify your own personal syndrome. Remember a syndrome does not necessarily equate to a disease, yet it can consist of a group of symptoms that may characterize a psychological disorder or other abnormal conditions that, truthfully, may influence all the critical decisions you will make throughout your life (I know it influenced mine).

Who is this book for? Or, who is the ideal reader of this book? The person reading this book is one who is feeling entrapped or who is experiencing being in a vicious cycle that they cannot seem to escape; one who questions why, despite their best efforts, they continuously find themselves making the same errors or decisions, or worse yet, repeating the same dreadful history. How will the reader benefit from reading this book? I firmly believe there are at least five benefits:

1. An increased or enhanced self-awareness
2. A burning desire to seek avenues for change
3. Better control or judgment in personal decision-making
4. Increased sensitivity or awareness to possible reasons for the actions of others
5. An ability to identify those elements that may serve as triggers to your syndrome

In addition to obtaining the above mentioned benefits from reading this book, I also feel that by observing and walking through the annals of my life along with me, you will learn how I was able to identify my own personal syndrome. You will also learn the spiritual tools I discovered and used to help me loosen the grip of my syndrome. You will also learn about the benefits I found in utilizing group and therapy sessions as well as how my faith in God proved to be instrumental in maneuvering the channels of my syndrome.

The origin of this book stems from the author's desire to provide a transparent look into his life and into how his personal syndrome affected all the areas of his life. Through his words he will provide the exact method by which his syndrome was unearthed and how he is now able to openly examine past decisions through the lens of his syndrome. He will candidly speak to both his successes and failures due to actions (and inactions) brought about by this syndrome.

Despite the lessons learned and the benefits gained from reading this book, let me tell you what this book is not. This is not an instruction manual, or a twelve-step program designed to assist an individual in overcoming his or her addictions or syndromes. One must understand that completely overcoming a syndrome is not possible. One can only seek to lessen the grip of your personal syndrome towards a fantastic existence. While there will be instances and incidents of overcoming, this book is not designed to highlight success stories, but to mirror life by giving a true account of both successes and failures. Although stories will be used to spotlight my syndrome at work, this will not be a "tell all" book, nor will it serve to display the sins of others, although some accounts will point out some sinful acts.

Have you ever known, or do you know of, anyone who has a fear of the dark? Have you ever been curious about what mysteries or untold stories may lie within the shadows of darkness? *Inside My Darkness* is a book that looks within to dispel the myths and misnomers typically associated with darkness. It is my hope that you embrace this journey, and it is my prayer that after you finish the journey along with me, you will develop a different respect, or even an appreciation, for darkness.

CHAPTER 1

PAIN...MY FOUNDATION

PAIN

by Courtney LaRoy Patterson

Hurt is the life-force within my
soul;
The wounds deepen as society
and I get old.
Being afflicted with illness throughout
my years;
My eyes are steadily filling with
aging tears.
As I tried to grasps life's
everlasting rope;
All seemed to be lost including

desire and hope.
Yearning for someone to give me
a helping hand;
I now realize my body shall return
to this dying land.
Though many people strive, still
others flee;
Nobody was here to receive the
bruises except for me.
Failure conquered me despite
my desperate try;
Maybe it's through fate that
I sit here and die.
Then will I see my beloved
and My Lord;
Never again to worry about
earth's devious hoard.
Life is simple, yet it is
tough;
but all was lost which still
is not enough.
The earth supports but seldom
tells the truth
But lack of love and pain is all
I obtain within my youth
My eyes are opened and
my horizons have lengthened;
I only hope that my desire
will soon strengthen.

What is pain? If I were to ask 100 people, I would probably get many variations as to what constitutes pain. However, I am sure the main [thread-woven] theme that would exist in all the definitions is "something that hurts." Well, I don't think that anyone would dispute that, but according to Merriam-Webster dictionary (now I did warn you that I had a few more definitions to give you), pain is "a basic bodily sensation that is induced by a noxious stimulus, is received by naked nerve endings, is associated with actual or potential tissue damage, is characterized by physical discomfort (such as pricking, throbbing or aching), and typically leads to evasive action." What? Simply put, it is something that hurts. Other definitions reference emotional distress or suffering, better known as grief. Whatever definition appeals to you, I can 100% guarantee that all living beings will experience some level of pain in their lives.

Of course, all types of pain have their variations. There is something we call "good pain," which seems oxymoronic—how can something that hurts be good? But bear with me for a moment. If you have done any type of exercise in your life, especially if you have not done so in a while, you will more than likely experience muscle soreness as a result of taxing those muscles. I have often heard people refer to that soreness as a "good pain," as it serves as evidence that you probably did something right in the gym. I know I have used that statement myself. The pain referenced in this book is far from what one can consider "good pain." In fact, my pain led to a desire to end my life, but more on that later.

How did pain become a life force, or a foundation, in my life? Unfortunately, I was an injury-prone child and routinely found myself in the emergency room. I appeared in the emergency room so much that the medical staff would ask "What did you do now?" whenever I'd come in. I don't know if that was out of exasperation or plain curiosity, but I wonder if the nurses and doctors were taking bets on how many times, I would find myself on that gurney at Normandy Hospital. Unfortunately, this injury bug would follow me well into my adult life, and the number of various injuries I've sustained throughout my life thus far is enough to fill the pages of a book on its own. Who knows? What would I title it—"*Pain and Me: A Lifelong Love Affair?*" Sounds intriguing, but I digress.

Like I stated, I will not bore you with all the injuries I suffered or the pain I endured; however, I find it important that I speak about one specific pain that would prove to be foundational in my life and present itself as the origin of my personal syndrome. I have named it the *blacker-than-me syndrome*. Don't worry; it will make sense here soon.

I was born in St. Louis, Missouri, at St. Louis City hospital on November 7, 1969, the first born to Connell and Cheryl Patterson. Later, I would find out that I was actually the second born to the couple, as my older sister had been stillborn only a year earlier. My first recollection of my life finds me in Seattle, Washington. From what I was told, my mother and father would divorce early on in my life and my mother, now a single mother with three children under the age of five, would try to carve out an existence and transport us between these two states, while she tried to "figure things out." I have some fond memories of living in Seattle; however, the memories that dominate my memory were traumatic in nature. Yet, these traumatic incidents would not be the cause of my syndrome.

Innocently enough, the incident that would spur this syndrome along happened when I was about seven years old, and my mother had decided that we would live in St. Louis permanently. During this time, my mother was still transitioning from Seattle, so it is unclear if she was in St. Louis along with us or still in Seattle, as there was a period that my siblings and I lived apart from my mother. Regardless, the whereabouts of my mother were not crucial to this incident, at least I thought.

We were living with my grandfather in Pine Lawn, Missouri, at, oddly enough, 4611 Seattle Street. A quaint and quiet neighborhood, it had a neighborhood park that was about a five-minute walk from the house. It being a relatively safe neighborhood, my brother and I were permitted to go to the park by ourselves. On this particular day, my Uncle Steve and his friends were also at the park playing basketball. Now let me quickly explain who my Uncle Steve is. Being the baby of his eight siblings, although he routinely would find himself in trouble up to his eyeballs, he was always given a pass by my grandmother. He was a dancer, a gymnast, a martial artist, and an artist, and seeing that he was only eight years older than I was, he was more like my big brother. I thought he was so cool, and I wanted to do everything he did, or so I thought. More on that later.

Normally, when we went to the park, we would usually go to the area where the swings, slides and merry-go-round resided. Or we might venture further into the park where the baseball fields were, to fly kites or play tag, but this day, since my uncle and his friends were in the park, my brother and I decided to hang around the basketball courts and observe the gameplay that was going on. Although we were just observers, one of my uncle's friends decided to acknowledge us. During those days, if you were acknowledged by the big kids, then you were among the cool. Being the nephews of Uncle Steve already gave us some level of notoriety, but this would take it to a new level. I don't even know if this kid (yes, he couldn't have been any older than fifteen) even knew our names, but when he spoke to us, he referred to me as "Hey, Blacker-than-me" and my brother as "Charleston Blue." I had no idea who Charleston Blue was, and still don't, but I guess he at least knew my brother's name was Charles. At first it didn't resonate with me, as I really did not realize that I was a dark-skinned kid; this was the first time in my life that attention was given to my complexion.

Figure 1:Charles (L), JJ (F), Me (R)

From the picture, you can see that I am a dark-skinned individual, but if it hadn't been for that insensitive kid, I probably wouldn't have realized this fact until a little later in life. As a side note, looking at this outfit, is probably the reason why I hate tank tops and plaids to this date.

Like I said earlier, his addressing me as "Blacker-than-me" did not initially resonate within my spirit, but unfortunately, a seed had indeed been planted. It didn't help that he kept cultivating that field within me by addressing me as "Blacker-than-me" every time he saw me. Soon, I lost my identity, and now I started noticing that I was indeed blacker than everyone around me, but I had no idea an unchangeable fact would alter every facet of my life. The power of one person's teasing words now defined me and soon set off the *blacker-than-me syndrome* that would control everything about me.

WHEN I CRIED...MY DARKNESS TAKES ROOT

WHEN I CRIED

BY COURTNEY LAROY PATTERSON

There were times that I cried and stayed
up all night.
wondering why I was cursed and wishing
I was right.
Curious why society would not accept
me.
Was it because of the dark past
within me?
But I was taught that my color

was a heavenly gift.
This somewhat gave my beaten
spirit a lift.
Many moon I stare and think
back
How much I truly hated being
black
Now my uttermost feelings are
weak and worn;
And my heart has been both
bruised, battered and torn.
Society has left me and
I cannot win
So I patiently wait for
my life to end.
There are many times I tried
to get life right
When I cried and stayed
up all night

Men are not supposed to cry! Shake it off! Crying is for the weak! Rub some dirt on it! (I never quite understood that one.) These were just some of the statements that were launched at me during my youth. Although this weird belief is common among males, it is especially prevalent among black males. Crying among black men is taboo, and even if you sustain a pretty serious injury (especially in sports), you better suck those tears in and find a way to push through that pain. No wonder there are so many of us that are messed up, but that's for another book. Up until the age of ten, my family and I would constantly move from house to house. I never really understood why we seemed to always be preparing to move, but it became the norm for me, or at least an expectation. Oddly enough, I can remember all our houses, mainly because I did something to get into trouble or something bad happened to me which punctuated my stay. Remember that my mother was a single mom, and it seemed like she always had a male friend who "tried" to be our father. I hated them all and I did everything in my little power to drive them away. For the most part I was pretty successful, but there was one guy named Roy who was like a cat and would always come back, even when a rambunctious ten-year-old threatened to hit him over the head with a lamp for touching my mother—in ANY way. Don't judge—I never said I was an angel, but he had that coming, I reasoned in my small adolescent mind. All of these men felt the need, or because they were dating my mom, felt obligated, to attempt to instill some manly wisdom into this rebellious child. I think some of that sunk into my younger brother, but I just outright rejected anything that emanated from their lips, even the word "hello." Oh, mind you, I constantly got into trouble for my rudeness and disrespect. Like they said, a hard head makes a soft behind, and I possessed the softest butt in the house.

In an article entitled "Tears and Black Masculinity," Jamar Boyd asks the question, "How does emotional expression prevent one from being a man?" I would be willing to bet that many men have asked the same question; nevertheless, we remain silent. With colonialism, the slave trade, centuries of slavery, Jim Crow laws, legalized segregation, mass incarceration, systemic racism, and unintentional bias all put in place to emasculate the black man, holding back tears through mental and physical pain appeared to be the only thing we had left to shore up our masculinity.

By the time I was ten, we had moved into a brand-new townhouse in a small ghetto city in the county of St. Louis named Wellston. According to my mother, during its heyday, Wellston was the place to be. With a bus station at the city's center and various stores lining the main street, people came from all over St. Louis proper to shop and hang out, whites and black alike. Yes, segregation was in full effect, but that did not stop Wellston from prospering. Now the city was a shadow of its former self. Although the bus station remained, it was tagged with graffiti from the warring gangs and it was no longer a place to hang out, but a stressful place to wait to transfer buses. Most of the stores were closed, abandoned, or boarded up, and those that remained were places one would go to get cheap gadgets, clothes, and trinkets and great barbecue, fish, and Chinese food. Side note: St. Louis has the best Chinese food and barbecue, bar none. Seeing that this is my book, there is no debate.

Once a growing metropolis and an economic center, Wellston was now characterized by a smattering of mom-and-pop shops, failing or dying industries, a plethora of liquor stores, sleazy motels that charged by the hour, street walkers (commonly referred to as hookers), gang warfare, drug dealers (and an equal number of users), and a growing number of Section 8 housing units, of which we would now become among the newest occupants. My family and I were among the first to move into the new townhomes in Wellston. In fact, we moved in before the complex was fully completed. When we parked in the parking lot adjacent to our house, it had yet to be paved and it was simply a dirt lot. Somehow, when my mom parked the car, the passenger door got jammed and didn't open and we had to climb out of the window, Dukes of Hazzard style (now I'm dating myself). Although there was no evidence of a collision, that door never opened again.

Wellston only had two schools, an elementary school that covered K through 8th grade and a high school. A middle school did exist down the street from the elementary school, but for some reason unbeknownst to me, it was shut down and all the kids now attended Central Elementary School. By this time the *blacker-than-me* syndrome was raging in my life. Moving from my grandfather's house on Seattle to our new house on Plymouth in Wellston, I had probably heard the *blacker-than-me* label at least two dozen times, and unfortunately it became synonymous with who I was becoming. I wouldn't understand or recognize this *blacker-than-me* syndrome for almost three decades later, but looking back, I can see it was in full control.

When that kid was addressing me as "Blacker-than-me," I soon began to believe that this also meant "less than me" as well. He didn't address any of the other kids my age by any demeaning names, and for some reason, everybody who was lighter than me in skin complexion (which was everyone) seemed to treat me differently now. I soon found myself playing in the park alone, spending time in the yard by myself, and slowly becoming a loner. By the time we moved to Wellston, I expected the same or worse treatment by the kids in the neighborhood, and lo and behold, they did not disappoint me. Even though the title would change to "blackie," "darkie," "spook" (you get the idea), the cumulative effect was still the same. In fact, it got to the point where I was beginning to hate myself because I couldn't change that one thing about me—my skin color.

Wellston was a pretty tough neighborhood, and the national pastime in this small city was boxing. At the local community center, a large majority of the boys in the neighborhood boxed, which meant that whether you signed up or not, you boxed as well, as those aspiring athletes were ALWAYS looking for a willing (or unwilling) sparring partner. During the bathroom breaks at school, it was Fight Club at Central Elementary and if your name was called you were up, whether you wanted to fight or not. And if you choose the latter, then you'd encounter a different boxing event after school. For some reason (please note the sarcasm), I was always one of the selected. I got pretty good at defending myself, and even better at taking a punch. And I took a lot of them.

Crying was forbidden in Wellston, and if you wanted to become a target, all you had to do was let someone see tears in your eyes. However, I was a target not because people saw me crying. For some unknown reason there existed a stereotype or misconception that the darker you were the fiercer you were, and many people wanted to test that, both inside and outside Central Elementary's bathroom. I fought a lot and was constantly afraid of just being me. At night when the day was done, I would ascend to my bedroom, climb into the top bunk in Charles' and my bedroom and cry myself asleep. No one would ever hear those cries but God, and unfortunately, He was not there to stand up to the bullies I would face on a day-to-day basis.

One day, I was down the street from my house playing with my friends, the Williamses. I can't remember exactly what we were playing, but all I know is that I was having fun. Now the Williams family was this family that consisted of single, twin mothers and their children living together under one roof. There were a lot of them, but they accepted me for some reason, and I didn't question why. Probably because many of the kids in the neighborhood picked on many of them, so maybe we had that misery in common, and like they say, misery loves company. At any rate, it didn't matter about the reason, all I know was on this particular day I was enjoying myself. As you have probably guessed, this happiness would be short-lived. At the time we were out in the street playing, one of their mothers and their next-door neighbor were sitting on the porch observing us. When I ran past them, I distinctly heard the neighbor say to Mother Williams, "That's an ugly black boy." Wow, what did this kid do to deserve that? So now grownups think that not only am I black, but I am ugly too?! So, that night, I ascended to my bedroom, climbed into the top bunk of my bed, and cried myself to sleep.

Strangely enough, this black, ugly kid appeared to have a way with the ladies. Well, at least I thought I did. To be honest, I am a very shy individual and that's a byproduct of my *blacker-than-me* syndrome: not wanting to be seen. But it seemed that I always had a girlfriend. Out of respect for them I won't name them, but if they read this book, they will know who they are, and if they tell the world I will deny them (just kidding). I had my first girlfriend when I was five—that's right, five—years old! Of course, I had zero idea what a girlfriend was at that age, but all I knew was that I spoke to this girl on the phone, and she appeared to like me, and I did like her. At this time, my Uncle Steve was dating her older sister and since he treated me more like a younger brother than a nephew, he "hooked" us up. I am sure he had ulterior motives, but I didn't care. V was my girlfriend, and I was on my way. Transparency moment: I never physically met V until I was about seven or eight years old. My uncle was still dating her sister and they were going to the drive-in (yes, I am dating myself again) to see the Chuck Norris film *The Octagon*. My uncle was a martial arts enthusiast and he worshiped Bruce Lee; since Chuck Norris trained under Master Lee, it made sense to go see this movie. Honestly, we could have gone and watched Lassie meet Godzilla and I wouldn't have cared. I was going to meet V for the very first time. When she entered the house, I couldn't believe how pretty she was. She was slightly older than me and just as shy. We exchanged pleasantries and sat as far apart as we could in the car on our way to the drive-in.

With my *blacker-than-me* syndrome in high gear, I wondered how she viewed me. Although my uncle and her sister would try to egg us on, we kept our conversation to a minimum, and as fate would have it, my Uncle Steve and her sister would eventually marry, but for V and me, our relationship ended at *The Octagon*. My next real girlfriend came along when I was eight years old and in the third grade. This relationship with G was special, and she was my first real kiss. I had never kissed before, and she knew this, but apparently, she had some experience with this because she questioned me, "Don't you know how to kiss?" I was mortified, but I tried to play cool, "Yeah I know how to kiss…." I certainly knew how to lie. Transparency moment: I must thank G for getting me to defend myself against a bully who was constantly taking my lunch money and making me steal on his behalf. She told me that if I didn't fight him that she would break up with me. Well, I ended up fighting this guy about eight times, and I beat him up every time. At that point I am not sure if I was doing it to appease her or because I enjoyed inflicting pain, but that is for another book.

This trend continued when we moved to Wellston, and I found myself dating M. Now M was unlike any of the girls I had dated in the past. She was, first and foremost, very developed, and this was indeed new to me. She was younger, whereas most of my girlfriends up to this point had been older than me, and the most noticeable characteristic was that she was very light skinned, completely opposite from me. I never stopped to wonder why I was attracted to this girl. Was it her build, or was it her complexion that somehow made me forget about mine? M and I didn't last very long, but then along came L. L had a darker complexion and was very thin and cute. She was younger than me as well. Strangely enough, L and M come right after one another in the alphabet and it just so happened that this L and M were best friends and lived right across the street from one another... drama! L and I dated for a while, and we would break up when C came along. C was the relative of the family down the street, who lived across from the Williams' home. She and I dated over the summer, but when she returned home to Illinois, I would fall prey to a rumor and we broke up, just in time for L and I to reunite and date again until I went off to college a couple of years later. So, having a girlfriend wasn't really an issue for me, yet I always wondered if it was a mercy thing, or if they truly desired me. If any of you are reading this book, I don't really need that question answered, I am not sure I can take it.

One day in the summer when we were out playing baseball, L and M were standing off to the side and I was playing catcher. Transparency moment: my mom told me that when I was a baby, I would routinely fall asleep with a bottle in my mouth. This trend continued even when I started growing teeth. According to my mother and dentist, I developed calcium deposits on my teeth that resulted in stains. To other people, it appears that I didn't practice good oral hygiene when, in fact, it was an issue beyond my control. Back to the story… L and M were talking to one another, unfortunately about me. Ever since the "That is an ugly black boy" comment had been uttered, I had developed a sixth sense when it came to people talking about me, especially if the term black was used. It is like everything else mutes and I can only hear that conversation. I heard M tell L, "He is cute, but his teeth are yellow." Goodness, now I am black and ugly *and* I have yellow teeth. I don't have a shot in this world, no matter how many girlfriends I may have had over the course of my life up to this point! So, that night, I ascended to my bedroom, climbed into the top bunk of my bed, and cried myself to sleep.

CHAPTER 3

THE DAY AN ANGEL FELL... FOUNDATION IS NOW SHAKEN

THE DAY ANGELS FELL
(DEDICATED IN THE MEMORY OF MY AUNT STEVELLA DICKSON)

BY COURTNEY LAROY PATTERSON

It was a lazy morning
in Milwaukee
As I lie asleep in a field
of dreams
I was awakened by a thunderous
voice aimed at me
Inquiring about the phone number
of a relative in St. Louis

The night before I had a dream
that my Aunt.....God's angel
Had taken a fall to her death
Driven aback from this thought
my soul shuddered from the grotesque
feeling
Leaving 5410w Concordia on my way
to the Laundry Mat
The undesirable thought seemed
to wash away
Like the soot within the woven fibers
of my clothes
Today, I along with my two siblings, would
depart for home
in
St. Louis
The farewells at the Greyhound
Bus Terminal were touching
As all departures are?!
The bus ride was pleasant and my
thoughts were numb.
Our arrival to St. Louis was
six hours later.
The greetings was joyful and gay
The ride home was admirable
Entering my house on Plymouth
my sight beheld:
Stan, Tracy, Shonnie, Demond and Zock
Then I felt my world crash
as I stood still in time

My nightmare had come true
God's angel did fall
And all she wore
were her panties and bra
Upon the cold floor
at
4868
Norwich
Place.

How can you love me so much to save my life but at the same time give up yours? My *blacker-than-me* syndrome was well established in my life by the time I was in my teens. Although I did not recognize it as a syndrome at that stage in my life, I knew that something was controlling me, and I let all those who interacted with me know it as well. As a dark-skinned child, I knew there was something different about me. I've heard that even before I was labeled as "blacker-than-me," grownups treated me differently. According to one account, when my family and I briefly lived in Milwaukee, Wisconsin and my mother and father were still together, I was severely beaten when a particular family member assumed that I was the cause of my younger brother crying. Now, mind you, I am eleven months, three weeks, and three days older than my brother, and during this time we both were babies. I don't know what I could have possibly done to spur any tears, yet this BLACK baby was responsible and had to be dealt with. While I cannot corroborate this incident, nor am I accusing anyone of mistreating me, I can say with impunity that Charles and I were treated differently.

With this knowledge firmly entrenched in my mind early in my childhood, I was a hellraiser. I was an angry, disrespectful, confrontational, depressing black hole (no pun intended). Whatever little positivity had been poured into me was lost and never reciprocated, and no one was able to reach this kid, except for one: Stevella Dickson, affectionately known as Aunt Stevie. Somehow, she knew how to circumnavigate the deep, dark waters of this kid and teach him to love back. While most adults dreaded seeing me coming, Aunt Stevie never reacted that way. When others decided to run away, Aunt Stevie would always run towards me. I was aware of people's disdain towards me, but I didn't care. Yet every day that would pass, I would think about how much I wanted to just die, at the tender age of eleven.

Aunt Stevie was what we could call a religious fanatic, and she LOVED God. Her reverence towards God was well known throughout the family, and when she entered the room people immediately took note and changed their tone. God was with her, and because of her, I soon realized God would be with me. One of the biggest tools I wield when it comes to dealing with my *blacker-than-me* syndrome is my faith. I know many of you have heard the saying "I grew up in church." Well, I can honestly say, I really did grow up in church. I started at a very young age saying Easter and Christmas speeches in my grandfather's church and eventually writing plays for my Vacation Bible School. I personally gave my life to Christ when I was about fourteen, yet God was with my family and me all my life. Because of Aunt Stevie, my family knew God.

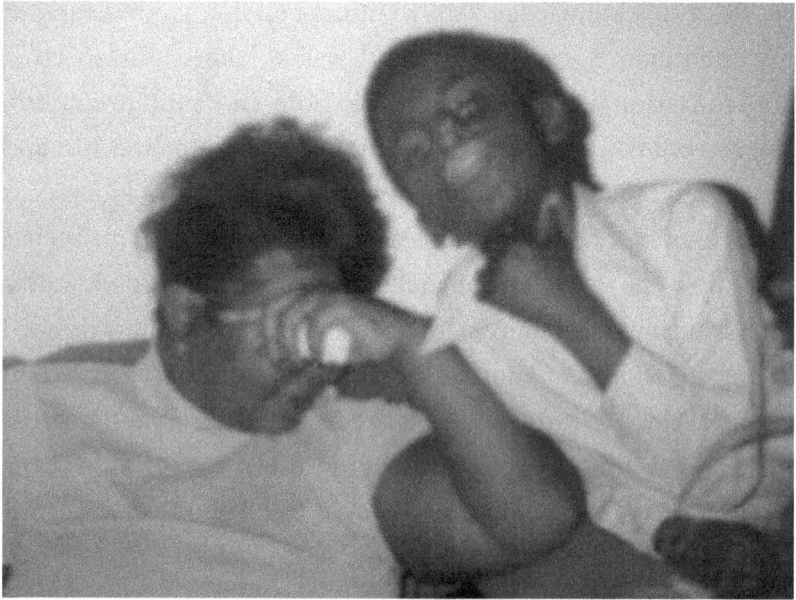

Figure 2: Aunt Stevie hiding her face and me

I have always had an affiliation with angels, and I personally met my guardian angel. Though it may sound like a fairytale and probably has a place in a fictional story, I first met my angel when we lived on Seattle prior to moving to Plymouth. Like I mentioned earlier in this chapter, I had begun to live a life of isolation. Being the oldest grandson and the oldest child in my immediate family, I really did not have any male role models. I know I mentioned how much I admired and worshiped my uncle, yet he never took interest in mentoring me or providing any guidance. Heck, he was a kid himself and he was too busy living his own wild lifestyle to take any interest in mine. Yet he was my hero…strange, huh?

I had strayed away from going to the park (for obvious reasons), and that day I was sitting on the porch steps with a football in my hand that I had gotten from one of my other uncles. Seemingly out of nowhere, this gentleman wearing sunglasses appeared on the other side of the hedges in the street. He inquired what I was up to and if I wanted to play catch. My mother had warned me to never talk to strangers, but in this instance, I felt comfortable with this individual. Maybe I was craving attention so much I didn't consider the danger this could impose. I embarrassedly informed him that I didn't know how to properly throw a football. He smiled and said, "I'll teach you." For about thirty minutes, he and I tossed the football back and forth. He showed me how to properly place my fingers on the strings of the football to throw the perfect spiral. Goodness, I was having fun!

After tossing the ball around, this gentleman then sat down next to me and talked to me about life, like a father would his son. Following our discussion he rose and said, "I'll see you tomorrow," and he disappeared down the street. The next day I sat outside in the front yard at the same time as the day prior, and just like clockwork, he appeared, still wearing sunglasses. This time I just hurled the ball towards him, and we began our bonding session. While throwing the ball, we both noticed I was not only throwing a better spiral, I was also tossing the ball a further distance. After about thirty minutes or so, we once again sat on the steps of the porch and talked about life. Although I can't remember in detail what we spoke about, all I know is that he was paying attention to only me and my skin color never came up in the conversation. Once again, this stranger rose after our talk and said, "I'll see you tomorrow," and yet again disappeared down the street.

I never told anyone about my new friend because 1) I was loving the attention, 2) I did not want to share, and 3) I was afraid that my mother or grandfather would stop me from interacting with this stranger. Day three came and there I was on the porch with football in hand, and like a perfectly tuned Swiss watch, he appeared, and we began tossing the ball again. Yes, my balls were traveling further, and my spiral was almost perfect. For another half hour or so I had a father, and I knew that when we finished, we would talk yet again. I so enjoyed our talks, our times together, and our bonding. This time we spoke a little longer and there was an increased seriousness in his tone. I was paying attention this time because he told me about being a man of faith and an overall good human being. I can remember shaking my head in agreement. This time when he rose to leave, he said, "I'll see you later." As a child, I translated that to "I'll see you tomorrow." So, I waved as he walked down the street and I disappeared into the house, enthusiastically waiting for tomorrow.

Day four, the next day, I appeared outside with my football in hand, eagerly waiting for my best friend to arrive. This time he was late...well, you can't be on time all the time. I waited and waited, but he never showed up. My excitement was immediately replaced with sadness, and I wondered if something I'd done the day before caused him not to show up. I couldn't understand what I had done, and I slowly dragged my dejected soul back into the house. Oddly enough, each day we were together out in the street, throwing the ball and talking, neither a car nor adult ever showed up to interrupt our moment together or distract from his message to me.

Just as mysteriously as this person arrived in my life, he vanished. As a kid, I couldn't help but think I was the cause of his disappearance. Did I demand too much of his time? Was I too needy? Did I suck at passing a football? I've often wondered if what really happened was that I received an angelic visitation. I would like to think so. It is no coincidence that he spent exactly three straight days with me. Could it have been Jesus Himself? Who knows? He appeared to Paul on his way to Damascus, and the Bible states that "He is no respecter of persons." Whoever he was, he threw a perfect football and had a cannon for an arm. Could this story be derived from the imagination of a lonely seven-, eight-, or nine-year old? Absolutely. But the one thing I have is evidence: I was never taught how to throw a football by anyone other than this mysterious individual, and even today I still throw a pretty good spiral. I'll let you be the judge. Transparent moment: my angel would once again revisit me several years later during an extremely dire moment in my life, but I will save that encounter for another book.

Speaking of angels, Auntie Stevie was indeed my angel here on Earth. She made me feel completely loved, and to be honest, I loved her more than anyone on this planet, including my own mom. To me, Auntie Stevie was flawless, and the disagreement that she had with my mother had to be my mother's fault, right? Auntie Stevie was the oldest of my grandparents' children and she was pregnant with her one and only child at nearly the same time as my grandmother was having her tenth. Aunt Stevie had her quirks (we all do), but to me they were endearing, and they were what made her *her*. I spent a lot of time over at her house, and she and I would sit in the back room and watch tennis on TV. I had no idea how this game was played, but if she liked it, I would learn to like it. She was my world at this time in my life, and it was solely because of her that I chose not to take my life one particular night.

In 1984, my life would change forever. In April of that year, my father contacted my mother to inform us that his mother, our grandmother, had passed away. Strangely enough, we had no relationship with her, so why was he calling? Later that night, my mother had told us that "Grandmother" had died and that my father wanted one of us to travel up to Milwaukee, Wisconsin, to represent her grandchildren at the funeral. I, being the eldest of the grandchildren from my mom, was 'voluntold' to attend the funeral. Despite my best protest, I was overruled. I would travel to Milwaukee with "family" on my father's side. I didn't even know that they lived in St. Louis, nor did I know them personally. Why would my mom send me away to a foreign place, with foreign people, to attend the funeral of a grandmother I didn't know and to represent the grandchildren, who had zero relationship with this lady or this guy? This was going to be a doozy of a trip, or so I thought.

It turned out the trip was pleasant, and the family treated me well and gave me applesauce-tasting hostess cupcakes (who invented those?). Soon we would reach Milwaukee, and for the first time since I was seven years old, I would come face-to-face with the man who was responsible for my being on this planet. I was now thirteen and deeply entrenched in my *blacker-than-me* syndrome. We would end up at a house where everyone was gathered and there I was, in a strange place surrounded by strangers who claimed to be my family. Soon there was a rustle and bustle in the crowd, and I overheard someone say, "Here he comes." The "he" they were referring to was my father, Connell Lathell Patterson, Sr.

When my father entered the house, there appeared to be an air of anticipation in everyone in the room except me. Since my *blacker-than-me* syndrome was in full effect, I was already feeling less than; why else would this man go nearly seven years without speaking or interacting with my family and me? If I had to categorize what I was feeling, I would say fear was the appropriate term. When he entered the place, there was a sort of celebrity reception for him that made that fear that was raging within me only grow. My father entered the room where I was sitting, and he approached me almost in slow motion. Soon he was standing right in front of me, and the place where I sat seemed ten degrees cooler due to the shadow he was now casting over me. With the room waiting with bated breath for what would be the first exchange between the two of us, this dude looked at me, wearing my newly purchased Michael Jackson 'Beat It' jacket, and said, "You think you are cool huh?"

My response: "What? Uh, no." And just like that, he had forcibly and unintentionally contributed to my *blacker-than-me* syndrome. Obviously, I reasoned, I wasn't good enough for him; how else could I explain how I managed to solicit such a response from a father who hadn't been there to watch me grow up or witness any of my successes and failures? But that is a tale for another day.

Chitchat was held at a minimum between us and eventually he, along with his wife, Audrey, would take me to his home where I would reunite with my older brother, Junior, and meet my stepsister, Lisa, for the first time. I would remain here for the remainder of my stay. Not surprisingly, the stay was relatively uneventful, and I had a decent visit. My father and Audrey would later drive me back to St. Louis in his custom Lincoln Continental adorned with the license plate "Satan 7." It should have been a warning.

When we arrived back home to St. Louis, the pleasantries between my mother and father were in abundance despite their tumultuous history. My father and Audrey would remain in our home for some time, and somehow, they convinced my mother to allow me, along with my siblings, to go up to Milwaukee for the summer. Because my earlier stay had been so pleasant, I became the biggest advocate for us to go, even becoming difficult for my mother to manage. Early on in our lives my mother would tell us of the horrible things my father had done to her and how he was a _____ (feel free to fill in the blank with whatever expletive and you'll probably be right). I would convince my siblings that Mom was wrong about our father. As we would soon find out, she wasn't.

Remember the license plate? When we arrived in Milwaukee at the beginning of that summer, I immediately knew something was amiss. For the entire time we were in Milwaukee, my father personified that person he paid homage to on the plates of his vehicle. The ultimate evil act would take place on a cloudy summer day, when what should have been a normal summer morning would be forever life-changing, at least for me. To offer clarity: prior to what my father would thoughtlessly do, I later found out that my mother had phoned him earlier and told him what occurred and begged him not to tell us, but just put us on a bus for St. Louis and she would tell us upon our arrival. She didn't want us to think about what happened during our travels. As you will see, that didn't occur. That morning my sleep would be abruptly interrupted by my father's bellowing voice. Still in the fog of sleep, I was peppered with questions about the phone numbers of various family members in St. Louis. Unable to gather any thoughts or remember any numbers, what my father said next got my total attention. "Courtney what's your Aunt Bonnie's phone number? I'm trying to find your mother; I'm sending you home; your Aunt Stevie is dead."

Sitting straight up, I asked, "What did you just say?" Just like a menacing parrot, he repeated what he had just said a minute ago. As I indicated in the poem that preceded this chapter, everything started moving in slow motion, even the trip home back to St. Louis on the Greyhound bus.

On the way home from picking us up at the Greyhound bus terminal, my mom and her boyfriend at the time, Mr. Richard, were somber. Once I entered the house, I knew that my earth angel's death was indeed a reality. I retreated upstairs to my room, and I would cry for hours until I drifted off to sleep on my tear-soaked pillow. My mother allowed me to not attend her funeral, and I remained at my Aunt Stevie's home, sitting just a few feet from the area where she died on the floor. Transparency moment: not too long before Aunt Stevie's death, I had a dream that she would die. Because I didn't know God the way I do now, when she died, not only did I feel that I was responsible for her death, but because I was in Milwaukee instead of St. Louis, I also felt additional guilt for not being there for her. She helped save my life and I felt I could do the same. My ONLY counter to my *blacker-than-me* syndrome was now dead, and I was completely lost. It would take almost two decades and years of therapy before I could muster the courage to visit the gravesite and apologize to her.

Figure 3: Auntie Stevie's Head Stone.

DARKNESS

CHAPTER 4

ANGER...MY NUMBER ONE CHARACTERISTIC

ANGER

BY COURTNEY LaROY PATTERSON

A force which engulfs the state of mind with irrational
thoughts and vengeful actions
Blood describes its character to such great
proportions.
Seething hot with treacherous wishes.
guided by the red mist which stains the eyes.
the force becomes a burden, causing the body
to harden.
An inescapable spirit which damages the innocent as well.

It has no aim but a main focus.
Like the eye of the tornado, everything, and everyone
becomes its victim.
No one escapes its grasp
Like a vice, the pressure is penetrating until....
It finally burst into a disheveled chaos destroying and
digesting everything within its path…

I have a firm belief that all syndromes produce byproducts. One byproduct may be sadness, or an obsession with food, drugs, or even sex. To be honest, the byproducts are endless. As for me, mine started off as sadness, because I didn't understand why people didn't like me, want to be around me, or simply accept me. As my *blacker-than-me* syndrome began to take root, this byproduct morphed into anger. The main catalyst for this metamorphosis was the simple fact that no matter where I went, kids seemed to want to fight me, just because of my skin complexion. Remember earlier I said that I fought a lot when I was a child, and it always seemed that the altercation was with the word "black" attached. This word would be screamed at me repeatedly throughout the fight—win, lose or draw.

The word *black* became a trigger for me. I became so sensitive to it that even in a crowded room, if anyone was having a conversation and the word "black" was spoken, suddenly all the sounds around me would become mute and I focused specifically on that conversation at hand, even though the conversation could innocently be describing the color of clothes, shoes, or whatever. As soon as the "black" word was uttered, I immediately felt that they were talking about me, and my defenses would go up.

In the beginning, others usually started the altercations resulting in the brawls, but as time went on, my anger caused me to become the aggressor. It started out with my siblings; they were easy targets. Later, I turned my attention towards those who I felt had syndromes that were "worse" than mine, at least so I thought. Prior to moving to Plymouth, my family and I had moved to various places throughout St. Louis city, only to return to my grandfather's house on Seattle. This time we moved to a quaint little house in Hillsdale, Missouri, a village within St. Louis County, which was oddly enough the neighboring city to Wellston, where we would eventually end up living approximately three years later.

Moving to a new home in a new neighborhood meant changing schools. With my *blacker-than-me* syndrome in tow, it wasn't long before I found myself the target of bullies and in several fights almost daily. In this neighborhood, however, there was a family that appeared to be the target of everyone's ire. In a low-income neighborhood, this family was the epitome of extreme poverty, and if that wasn't enough, they were from a single mother household, like many of the families were. Unfortunately, the mother was one who was a true religious zealot, who publicly abused her children in the name of Jesus. Not only were these kids constantly being attacked by the kids in the neighborhood, but they also had to worry about whether they would receive a beating from Mom, who always seemed to be on the phone talking about God. All this just because they were extremely poor.

One day after school, there was a large group of kids encircling some girls. I could tell by the commotion that someone was involved in a fight—ah, what a familiar sight. As the crowd moved down the street, I could see that this mob of kids was attacking these girls. What could they have possibly done? Immediately I realized that these girls were being mob attacked because they looked different due to their poverty syndrome. I was suddenly empathetic to their plight. However, that empathy was short-lived, as the crowd had now moved to where I was standing and immediately, I was immersed in the crowd. Call it mob mentality, but I found myself standing before the eldest of the trio. In that instant, there existed a battle of syndromes: theirs vs. mine. For fear of the crowd latching onto my syndrome I decided to keep the focus on hers, and I began to launch my own verbal attack towards this person that did nothing wrong to me, and of course I did not stop there, so to keep the spotlight trained on her syndrome I did the unthinkable and struck her in the stomach.

From all the beatings this young lady had suffered at the hands of her mother and probably a litany of kids over the years, her body had hardened in an effort to protect her from assaults. So, when my fist connected with her belly, it was so muscular and hard that she absorbed my punch without so much of a flinch, and I immediately regretted my actions. "I'm sorry," I began to plead. Transparency moment: since my mother suffered domestic violence at the hands of my father, she raised me not to hit women, so I wasn't sure if I was apologizing because I was being sincere or was afraid she would in turn destroy me. The look in her eye seemed to indicate that she knew that I had hit her from the depths of my own syndrome, and she signaled, "I forgive you!"

Despite that day of reckoning, I was still a hellraiser, and many of my family members seemed to hate it when I came around. My syndrome-driven anger caused me to terrorize my brother and sister, disrespect my elders, and try to fight my mother's male friends, multiple times. Surprisingly, I felt justified in all I was doing, and I don't know how I survived those years, but by the grace of God.

I would love to conclude this chapter with a counter story of how I beat this anger thing and now I am a patriot of and a staunch believer in non-violence, but that couldn't be further from the truth. Remember I said that the byproduct of my *blacker-than-me* syndrome is anger, so undoubtedly, I encountered fits of rage, as I had described in this chapter; however, since I have discovered the origin of my syndrome, I feel I am more in control of what I do with this emotion. When my *blacker-than-me* syndrome tries to indicate to me that I am "less than," I use this message and attempt to use that energy of my anger to fuel and propel me towards success. This exercise has allowed me to garner wins in my professional, personal, and public endeavors. Some of these successes I will share in subsequent chapters. Another transparent moment: still today I deal with this potentially destructive force, and I try to transform this into an action that builds up instead of tearing down, and it is a lot of work that I still struggle with. Yet because I now know where this comes from, I can place my energy towards a positive outcome instead of a negative one. This is a possible task, albeit not an easy one.

CHAPTER 5

WHAT...THE REASON

"WHAT?"

BY COURTNEY LAROY PATTERSON

My vision was blurred by the cold mist
of the morning sky. The bright colors
surrounded me, teasing me, mocking
me like children at play.

Beyond, there stood some figures
whose faces I could not identify. As
they started to move towards me their
face became shallow and dark like that

of an evil swamp or lagoon. They did
not speak but moved steadily with the
agility and speed of nature's finest
creatures.

Frightened by their ominous gait, I
attempted to flee with the atmosphere
grabbing my heels, taunting me,
permitting me not to run.

As I stood there a bridge appeared out
of the thickness of the night. Its path
lead to the valley of no return and no
color. Lead by instincts alone, I

managed to mount the bridge expecting
the worst. My expectations did not
falter because the bridge collapsed and
I plunged headfirst into that deep

dark terror below me and at that
moment I encountered............

I've always considered myself a dreamer. When Aunt Stevie
was alive, she would always say to me that I possessed the gifts
of revelations. Focusing on the Book of Revelation in the Bible,
I thought this meant that I possessed the power to see into the
future. Well, I was partially right in that the gift of revelation
does just that—reveal things. This could be things happening in
the future, but it can also reveal current events or make sense out

of past situations. Whatever the time frame, the person receiving this revelation is indeed edified. As for me, my gift was in the sphere, or area, of revealing things in the future, which is why I was deeply devastated at the death of Aunt Stevie: because I saw it occurring just months before it would happen. Throughout my life, a large majority of the dreams that I can readily remember often came true. Many people often refer to this as déjà vu, or the feeling of having already experienced a present situation. I have typically referred to my déjà vu moments as God providing guideposts to assure me that I am on the correct path. Normally, I dream in color, and only a few times in my life to date have I dreamt in black and white. But because this was so rare, I wondered what something like this could mean.

According to an article on the website Liquids and Solids, black and white worlds don't exist, even though what is taking place may appear real to us. As a website that seeks to focus on spirts, dream, symbolism, and giving an explanation for everything, the authors of the article give eight spiritual meanings that black and white dreams may contain. I will spare you the entire list in this book (I will provide a reference to the article in the notes if you desire to learn all eight spiritual meanings), but I will focus on the two spiritual meanings that I see completely applying to my life. According to this article, the first of the spiritual meanings that applies is that I could have been "feeling lonely, grieving a loss, or just feeling disconnected." With my *blacker-than-me* syndrome in full effect, feeling lonely or feeling disconnected was a normalcy in my life. As one yearning for companionship or seeking to just be loved (or even liked), my efforts to fit in were almost always thwarted, causing me to turn in on myself.

My initial black and white dream occurred prior to Aunt Stevie's death, therefore the loss of a loved one was not yet applicable to my life (boy, that would change...).

Just like anyone else, I desired to fit in, but when those "Hey Blacker-than-me" words were uttered in my youth, the separation from others began. Not only was I no longer going to be accepted by my peers, but I would also start losing my place within my family. I felt ostracized at school, at home, on the playground, and on the street. Oddly enough, the only places I felt a sense of belonging were at Aunt Stevie's home and in church. Even in my own home among my immediate family, I no longer felt like I belonged. To illustrate this feeling I was having, my mother had on her wall a family photo consisting of her, my brother Charles, and my sister Sharhonda. Of course, I am obviously absent from this photo. Each time I see that picture, to this day, I am reminded that at least on that specific day, I did not belong. I don't remember where I happened to be at the time of that photoshoot, but I do know that for some reason, in that photo they all looked happy to me. Yes, that is my *blacker-than-me* syndrome talking.

Dreaming in black and white can also signify feeling that one is not in control of one's life. Understand that being a kid, I wasn't supposed to be in control of my life, but as I began to get older, not being in control became synonymous with who I was becoming. This feeling of loss of control and loneliness was best exemplified in the first black and white dream I had when I was eight years old.

The setting for this dream was in our small house in the city of Hillsdale, Missouri. I was returning home from school, but for some reason I was alone. I immediately sensed that something was wrong because Charles, my younger brother, and I normally traveled to and from school together. Although I can't recall what time of the year it was, when I entered the house, there was a chill in the air. We didn't have central air conditioning, so I was unclear where this cold air was coming from. Moving from the living room into the next room (I believe it was the dining room), the house seemed bigger than usual. I began to call out to my family. "Mom, Charles, Sharhonda!" Silence. Since it was totally uncommon for any of the kids to be home alone, when I did not get any response, my first instinct was to look for my family.

Against my better judgment, I ventured further into the house. The rooms were darker than usual, and the deeper I went inside the house, the colder and draftier the house became. Opening an unfamiliar door, I entered a room where I could see what looked like items hanging from the ceiling. A faint stream of sunlight (at least I can say it was daylight) entered the room. Upon closer examination, the items took on the shape of human bodies, except they were not actual bodies, just their skins, albeit still intact. As these human skins came more into focus, I could see several of them hanging from the ceiling, again just the skins and no bodies attached. Even without the bodies, I could detect distinct features on each of the faces. As more light began to fill the room, it became littered with what seemed like dozens of these skin-like things dangling from the ceiling like Christmas ornaments. Because I didn't recognize any of the people, I didn't know whether these were the actual skins that were removed from a person's body.

Taken aback from this discovery, I did not notice any foul smells in the home, yet I was scared, but my desire to find my family intensified when I suddenly realized that, outside of these dangling skins, I was in this house alone. But this was our home… or was it? The rooms did seem familiar, altered slightly, and there were things present inside the room that I clearly recognized. I decided to return to the front of the house to wait for my family to come home. What I would see next would incite instant fear.

Returning to the front room, I once again noticed these skins hanging from the ceiling. "How did I not notice these earlier?" I said to myself. This time, when I inspected these skins, I stood in shock as I identified the skins of my family among this group of what can only be deemed as prizes or trophies. But who or what would do this? And more importantly, why? Outside of an audible gasp, I remained speechless. In horrified disbelief, I continued to stare at my family hanging there. "Did this just happen?" my eight-year-old mind tried to reason. "How did I not hear anything?" the conversation continued.

Now, shadows are normally dark and ominous in regular dreams, but in a black and white dream the contrast is so stark that its effects are multiplied. Suddenly, out of the shadows emerged this figure, which can only be described as a combination of the caricature of the Tasmanian Devil from Bugs Bunny and Venom, the villain from Spiderman. If you have no idea what I am referring to, this would be a great time to do a Google search for both characters and allow your imagination to stitch them both together. Whatever you come up with, you'll be right.

Unexpectedly, this terrifying creature lunged at me, and in what can only be classified as a supernatural feat, I jumped back, narrowly escaping its sharp claws, and now there existed a twenty-foot gap between the creature and me (I told you the room was unusually large) and I began to run, with this thing in chase. Now when I get to heaven, I am going to ask God why we run so slow in dreams (not to mention I was on eight-year-old legs). As I made my way to the front door, my adversary was quickly narrowing that gap. Upon reaching the door, I had to muster up the strength to open it and by now, what I dubbed as the "skin monster" was a mere few feet from me. Busting out the door, I tore down the stairs and breached the front yard gate with the skin monster on my heels. This is where this strange nightmare gets weirder.

Off in the distance, across the street, my dream changed into color. Although I was still running in a black and white state, instinctively I was trying to reach the color. As I got closer to the area where black and white transitioned to color, I could feel the skin monster's hot breath on my neck. In one last effort to get me, he reached out, grabbing my shirt, and at the moment he finally got a hold on me, I stepped across the street into color. The skin monster instantly let go of me, retreated, and darted back into the house where the skins of my family and others were hanging, but I kept running in my newly found escape route until I finally woke up.

I've only told a handful of people about this dream in the details that you read in this chapter. For those few I did share this nightmare with, typically I would give a summary of the dream, but I told my earthly angel, Aunt Stevie, the colorful details, no pun intended, about this dream. In her religious zealot fashion, she informed me that it was a sign that the devil was trying to get me, and she may have been right. But am I to believe that he already had possession of my family? That was hard to stomach.

I never really sought an explanation for this dream, and as you can see, I still remember it in vivid detail almost fifty years later.

Transparent moment: I must admit that I never went to God about the meaning of this dream for fear of what He would reveal. Unfortunately, the God that I was introduced to in church from my youth was a punishing one, and although He sent Jesus to redeem us for our sins, God and judgment were synonymous with one another; therefore, any revelation of this dream, I felt, had to be some type of punishment or judgment being enacted. But what I recently discovered is that this God is not the God of the Bible. Yes, there are stories in the Bible where He did deliver swift punishment or judgment, but the God of the Bible is a God of love and compassion, and through the writing of this chapter, He revealed to me that I must move away from the dogma of my *blacker-than-me* syndrome and stop seeing life in a monochromatic way.

God also wanted me to realize that He has provided colorful moments in my life to combat the evilness of my blacker-than-me syndrome, and for this dream to serve as a stark warning that if I ventured back into that house of my syndrome, that the skin monster is always there awaiting my return. When I wrote the poem "What," I was unclear on what type of obstacles stood before me. As I was coming into my own as a young man, I did not know what was expected of me or, more importantly, what could possibly happen to me. Like all of your lives, my life has taken unexpected twists and turns and I have faced the wrath and ire of some simply because of my skin complexion. As I was beginning to understand the "What" that led to the origin of so many things I would encounter, my maturing mind was still wrestling with the "'Why."

DARKNESS

CHAPTER 6

WHY...A PERPETUAL QUESTION

"WHY?"

by Courtney LaRoy Patterson

Why is there hunger
when food is plenty?
Why give aid to Russia and
not give the poor any?
Why bus kids to the county
when good schools are near?
Why run from gangs when
it's the police you fear?
Why pray to God and
commit unforgettable sins?
Why get caught cheating and

let your marriage end?
Why steal from your family
with a gun or knife?
Why use drugs, kill your
children or beat your wife?
Why are there revolutions
battles and wars?
Why are there expensive,
small and imported cars?
Why are there unemployed
homeless and horrible lives?
Why is the fortune of a
person killed when stocks
dive?
Why is there death, murder
or suicide?
Why is death in a car called
vehicular homicide?
Why are women beaten,
bruised and endlessly
raped?
Why won't Congress pass
laws as means of escape?
Why do taxes avoid the rich
and force the poor to give?
Why, honestly, is there
nothing that gives any
reason to live?

WHY... A PERPETUAL QUESTION

Have you ever doubted or questioned the actions of God? What about asking, "God, why are you doing this to me?" or "God, why is this happening to me?" We all have done this at some point in our lives. The longer I walked with God, the more I realized that God really doesn't "do" anything to us, but permits things to happen to us, mainly for our own benefit and often for Him to gain His glory. At the height of my *blacker-than-me* syndrome, I often said to God out of my frustration, "Lord, why did you make me this color?" Of course, He never provided an answer that I could readily accept (yes, God speaks to me, and if you allow it, He'll speak to you as well). Several years after I wrote the above poem "Why," the group 3T, nephews of Michael Jackson, came out with a song with the same title written by Kenneth "Babyface" Edmonds, my favorite singer. The song featured the King of Pop singing with his three nephews, Tariano, Taryll, and Tito, hence 3T; in the chorus of the song the singers pose some practical 'why' questions with no simple answers:

"Why does Monday, come before Tuesday? Why do summers start in June? Why do winters come too soon? Why do people fall in love when they are always breaking up? Oh why, why do we love when love will die?"

The song goes on to repeat a similar stanza that concludes with a why question that I often wonder if God Himself asks about us:

"Why do I love you? Tell me why."

When I look at the current state of this world, I don't know why you love us either, Lord, but that is what makes God, God. As I am writing this chapter, the airways are filled with the news of back-to-back mass shootings taking place in California, with approximately eighteen innocent people losing their lives. As my heart grieves for these families, the question 'why' continues to swim in my head. It should be natural to have those 'why' questions when tragedies like that described above transpire; however, we tend to dwell on this question even when we experience mundane mistakes such as dropping things although we have thumbs designed to prevent this! Why?!

Transparency moment: I personally hate cheese, and no, this isn't a byproduct of my syndrome; I just detest it. So, tell me why, when I order a hamburger, must I request no cheese? Now I think I'm a pretty smart guy, so to me the word 'hamburger' denotes no cheese since there exists a word called 'cheeseburger' which, to me, is self-explanatory. I am confused by this, and I spend a lot of time doing laps in the drive-through to get a hamburger. Please pray for me.

I did tell you that I would provide tools that will aid you in loosing the grip of your personal syndromes. I have spent the first several chapters of this book highlighting a specific tool due to its importance. This tool is simply *acknowledgement*. Being able to overcome, defeat, or in this case, overpowering the grip of one's syndrome or an addiction is accomplished by first acknowledging that a problem *does actually* exist. We as humans are so quick to deny our own faults—and equally as quick to point out the faults in others—that we often miss the thing that is hindering us. Jesus was quick to denounce these actions, as it was recorded in Matthew 7:3 (NKJV) where He asks, *"And why do you look at the speck in your brother's eye, but do not consider the plank in your own eye?"* Guilty as charged!

The tool disclosed in this chapter has proven extremely instrumental in my successful in overcoming the grip of my syndrome. Remember the house in Hillsdale that was the scene in my dream with the 'skinmonster'? Well, there was our neighbor's house, which was a well-kept and manicured ranch style house. It was blue with white trim, and it had a white picket fence enclosing the yard, making this corner house so picturesque, it should have been on the cover of a home and garden magazine. Although I can't remember all the inhabitants of this house, the one person I can remember would affect my life for years to come. L (this is a different L) had to be between eight and ten years older than I was, which would have made him practically grown to us. He was very friendly to the kids around the neighborhood, and he often interacted with D, my other next-door neighbor and best friend at that time, as well as me. One day, D and I were in L's backyard playing. It was fun, and for a fleeting moment I didn't feel judged, and I felt completely accepted. I can't remember what game we were playing but everyone appeared to be enjoying themselves, especially L, who was taking turns between D and me, doing what can only be described as physically violating us. It was conducted in such a way, however, that I didn't view it in that light.

The laughter that was coming from D only made me think he felt the same way, but I could have been wrong. This back and forth didn't last very long. Maybe L had his fill, or it was getting late, but we eventually left his yard and went home. Strangely enough, D and I never spoke about this even though I know we were both affected by it. That was the only time that I can remember L having both of us together, but I distinctly remember L had me alone in that backyard on a subsequent visit. As he continued to grope between my legs, I can remember laughing the way I

heard D laughing the last time he and I were together with L.
Did I enjoy it? Did I laugh because L was expecting me to? Was
I afraid and used laughter to mask it? Did I hope my laughter
would eventually make him stop? I really don't know. Yet there
is one thing I do know: what he did to me would affect me well
into my adult life. I now reason that it was my *blacker-than-me*
syndrome that silenced my voice and prevented my resistance.

I believe that the more I think back on those days, I can
remember times that I questioned my own masculinity. I never
thought that I was gay or anything like that, but because of
what happened to me, I did feel part of my masculinity was
compromised. This destructive thought would only be exacerbated
when I would get propositioned by gay men. What type of vibe
was I giving off to be approached so often? I guess I was just
in the wrong place at the wrong times. God only knows. Even
though I was now married, I didn't realize how much disdain I
held towards L for the role he played in causing me to call into
question the levels of my very own masculinity. This realization
came about when I attended the program in my church called
"Life Hurts; God Heals." It was during this course that I realized
that what I had begun calling my *blacker-than-me* syndrome was
telling me, "Remember you are less than," and here was L, this
light-skinned individual, giving me that attention I craved. Of
course, what he was doing was wrong, but at least I was getting
the attention that was missing in my life. Sad. Lord! Was I that
lonely that in exchange for attention I would allow my body to
be violated, and by a guy, nonetheless? I was seething with anger,
but who was I mad at? Him for doing this to me, myself for

craving attention so bad as to forgo self-dignity, or was it God for seemingly abandoning me? I wasn't sure; I was simply mad.

There came a part in the program where the attendants had to bring several rocks to the class. They had to be large enough so you could write someone's name on them. With *my blacker-than-me* syndrome controlling the narrative, I went and found some decent sized ones, not knowing what they were for, but if we had to throw them at something or someone, I was ensuring I would stand out. There is some irony here, because for this exercise we were instructed to write the names of all the people we had unforgiveness towards, and each rock represented a person. Okay, done, no damage done there. Naturally, L's name appeared upon one of the rocks. To my surprise, when I began writing down names of those people who had hurt me to that point, there was soon such a litany of them that I ran out of rocks. Goodness, did I harbor that much unforgiveness? Yet each of them had something to do in part with my *blacker-than-me* syndrome, including my mother. More on that later.

Sitting behind my makeshift rock garden, I wondered what we would do with these named rocks. As I began to focus my attention elsewhere, I was handed a burlap sack. We were then instructed to place these rocks into that bag. "Man, this is going to be heavy," I thought. "Carrying this is going to be a beast," I snickered to myself. I felt sorry for that poor soul. At the conclusion of the class, we were told that for the next week we would have to carry this bag of rocks wherever we went. "You have to be freakin' kidding me!" I exclaimed. I quickly realized that the poor soul would be me. Had I understood what this phase of the exercise would consist of, I would have only gathered some pebbles and just placed initials on them. Now I was stuck carrying this Santa Claus sack from hell around with me for a week. This bag represented the baggage of unforgiveness that we all carry around with us daily, and the sole purpose was to feel the weight of these burdens.

I took that sack of rocks with me everywhere I went—to the store, to work, literally everywhere. I don't know what was worse, lugging those rocks around or the looks I received as I safeguarded a bag of rocks. As the week went on, I began to detest this bag of rocks. It was cumbersome, dirty, and, of course, heavy, and they got in the way of EVERYTHING I wanted to or tried to do. I could not wait to get rid of them. I got the message. I understood the burden of carrying around unforgiveness. But the next phase in this exercise changed my perception of unforgiveness forever.

After a week of dragging this bag of rocks around, we were then directed to find a large body of water to cast these rocks into as an **act of forgiveness**. Once these rocks were tossed into the water, they were never to be retrieved again, and the ill feelings that were represented in placing those names upon those rocks were to go along into the water with them. I took a trip to the Quincy Reservoir near my home here in Colorado with my big bag of burdens. I found a nice quiet spot near the back of the reservoir and started the process of forgiveness. This action would take over an hour to complete. I would reach inside the bag and retrieve a rock. Once I read the name, I would recall the situation, say a prayer, declare to the heavens that I forgive them, and then throw that stone as far as I could into the water symbolizing the sea of forgetfulness as spoken about in the Bible. This was a powerful exercise, and it did take some time to complete based upon how many stones one had. There was no set pattern since you had no idea who would emerge from the bag next.

One by one, I would grab the rock, relive the incident, pray for forgiveness, discard the stone, and repeat the process. Eventually I would pull L's stone. I did not hesitate but went immediately into my forgiveness prayer. I prayed a little bit longer for L; maybe a little of that was for me as well, and I don't doubt that I threw his rock the farthest, but I had no way of knowing. I often wonder if I was visualizing throwing L into that water, which would explain the incredible energy behind the toss.

Transparency moment: this was a spiritually, mentally, and physically taxing exercise. I left the reservoir noticeably drained, and I couldn't wait to get home and take a nap. Returning to the class later that week, we had to speak about one of those stones and how difficult the exercise was. I spoke about L. Although I had forgiven him before God at the reservoir, I felt I also needed to forgive him before man, which is what I did. And if by chance you pick up this book and recall what you did to me, I will now tell you that I do and did forgive you.

Forgiveness is a powerful tool to use to overpower the grip of one's personal syndrome. You will need this to help move past painful memories that feed your syndrome. Forgiveness allowed me to deal with those people who sought to remind me of my syndrome and to rise above intentional acts that aimed to hurt me because of my complexion. Forgiving requires a lot of energy to execute, but this energy does not compare to the energy you will expend dragging those rocks of unforgiveness around every day. Don't take my word for it, try the exercise that I described earlier in this chapter. The energy you regain from forgiving people will provide much-needed fuel to propel you beyond the reach of your syndrome as it tries to continue keeping you in the belly of the beast. Now I would be lying to you if I said that I don't think about some of the things that L did to me. Unfortunately, in this world there are triggers, but unless I want to return to the reservoir, jump in, swim to the bottom, and locate that specific rock and reinstate his unforgiveness, L's forgiveness remains intact. Sometimes when I think about these incidents in my life, I find myself having out-of-body experiences, and I'm able to view my life through the eyes of someone else. This gives me a different perspective and I can sometimes understand the actions of others. This doesn't mean I condone making anyone feel less than, yet I kinda get it. When I have this out-of-body experience, I feel it's a middle passage moment for me, akin to when the first slaves were brought to this country to have their lives brutally changed...forever!

CHAPTER 7

MIDDLE PASSAGE...A SYNDROME REVEALED

MIDDLE PASSAGE

BY COURTNEY LAROY PATTERSON

The plight of the black man
is both hard and rough
You've stolen our pride...raped our women
Now tell me, isn't that enough?
But I sailed across your Atlantic
Bound and chained upon your boat
Through the waves your voice kept saying,
"Now see if this nigger can float."
All around...I felt

the soul and the screams
Wondering about our fate
beyond any of my wildest dreams.
I pleaded with my brothers
and counseled with my sisters
You came below deck
addressing us as slaves....yourself-MISTER
You flaunted your power with
such style and grace
But when I asked you a simple question
Your fist was slammed into my face.
When we landed, I met
chains, sticks, and was whipped
My brain now shackled and
my freedom...now clipped
I was stripped from my home
and shipped to this land
I was beaten, bruised and humiliated
with nothing but your tools in my hands.
I saw the others fight
I saw even more flee
But in the end of the chaos
You blamed the revolt on me.
My people were hanged
done before my face
You stood there with your Sunday suit on,
your women dripping with lace.
I screamed for my mother
who's in Kenya...my home
I looked around-we're in hundreds

yet I feel so alone.
You raped our mother…Africa
of her resources…her gold
"We are only here to preserve it"
Is the story you often told.
You gave us new identities
Even gave us new names
But my love and heritage from Africa
Will forever remain the same.
You befriended me and insulted me
But look………I did not cry
You killed many of my brothers and sisters
and you can choose how I shall die.
You banished our rituals
You have disgraced my race
I now see you're integrating
try to change the color of our face.

Growing up in the 80s, as a young man, if you were not light-skinned and bow-legged, you didn't have a prayer when it came to attracting females, at least as far as I could tell. Seeing that I was neither and that I was very shy, for the life of me, how did I manage to have one girlfriend, much less the number of companions I possessed over the years? To be honest, I don't think I ever asked any of them to be my girlfriend, although I have some recollection of being asked at least once to be a boyfriend. Now that I reflect on this, I don't even believe I asked my current wife to go steady when we began dating. So, it appears that pattern continued into my adult life. While girls were "ga-ga" over these bow-legged light-skinned brothers, at the same time there was an emerging trend at aiming to get connected with your "blackness," which translated into a pride for your African roots. Red, green, and black colors found on the African flags seem to be found everywhere in the black culture, and African medallions found their way around the necks of prominent blacks as well as those of us looking to simply embrace our African roots. With these two competing narratives in effect, for the first time in my life I felt a sense of belonging; however, I was unaware that this divide within the black race has never been seen since the intentional division that was instituted between the slaves. Now, here I was in the midst of a complexion war within my race.

In a 2014 study by Uzogara et al., it was determined that within African American culture, skin tone became an important characteristic used to create division within the community as well as affect the quality of life of the community's inhabitants. These authors continue their study by stating that not only did skin tone conjure up division in the black community, but it also became a source of judgment. I can hear the defenders now: "That doesn't apply to me; I don't see color," or "I am not a judgmental person." I apologize, but both of those statements are false.

Just like we all have syndromes, everyone passes judgments as well, be it consciously or unconsciously. Undoubtedly, other races use skin tone to pass judgment against black people; however, this usage is noticeably different among blacks. For example, when a white person encounters a black person, the skin tone conjures up an interaction with a black person first, and then the type of skin tone may come into play. For blacks, the skin tone is all that registers. I know a percentage of readers of this book will try to debunk this, and if by some miracle of God you are successful, then I applaud you, because you can be among the first to fulfill Dr. King's wish that his children are judged by the content of their character and not by the color of their skin. Dr. King, I, too, have that dream.

Sorry, back to my story. Here I am in college, all militant up in my African garb, with Public Enemy's *Fight the Power* as my theme song. As hard as I was trying to present myself as this unmovable black force, to personify this, I enrolled in a poetry class. Oh, the irony! As tough as I tried to present myself, I found that persona difficult to maintain when I was focusing on my iambic couplets or trying to master a haiku (poetry talk, guys). Oh well, at least my Africa medallion was prominently worn, and I paraded the red, black, and green colors with pride.

Being the only black in poetry class, I would soon realize that being the only "darkie" present would become a major theme in my life due to my *blacker-than-me* syndrome. I did all I could to establish myself as a prominent black, while there was a growing divide among the various shades of blacks across the college campus. Around this time, Spike Lee's film *School Daze* was playing in theaters all over the world. In an iconic scene reminiscent of West Side Story, you had two embattled groups of girls. There were the dark-skinned soul sisters with natural hair and no makeup, who were disparagingly called "Jigaboos" by the fair-skinned, long straight-haired, attractive popular girls whom they referred to as "Wannabes." In this scene, the two groups of girls lob insults and stereotypes at one another, all the while trying to outperform the opposing girl. As this bantering between these two distinct groups was taking place on the silver screen, I watched this play out in real life on my college campus. So now I was a jigaboo because of the coat of skin I was born with? Nah, I refused to take that title on board.

Realizing that most of my fellow students in my poetry class would never see *School Daze*, I never had any fear of being labeled a jigaboo, much less explaining what one was. Yet, I felt compelled to prove that I was not one in the eyes of my classmates. Ironic, seeing that this word is simply a derogatory term to describe a dark-skinned individual. I wrote many poems in this class, some you've had the opportunity to read in this book, but the poem that heads this chapter would garner an unexpected response from both my teacher and classmates. During this period in the class, we were instructed to write a poem in a specific format. In this format we had to write a poem from the standpoint of viewing our lives through the eyes of another. Because I was now identifying with the "mother" country, I made the decision to write from the perspective of an African making the journey to the Americas to spend his life as a slave, hence "Middle Passage" was created.

After I finished the poem, I was asked to recite it before this class. Mustering my inner Eddie Murphy "Kill the White People" tone, I read that poem like I was in a Black Panther rally, with the pace and fervor of Malcolm X. After I completed my spill, there was dead silence for what seemed like an eternity (probably was thirty seconds in reality). I thought to myself, "Aw, hell, I just insulted the entire classroom!" Suddenly, that militant Courtney was gone as fast as he came. As if it was choreographed, the entire class began clapping in unison, for at least five minutes. The teacher couldn't stop giving me compliments after compliments. Truly a twilight zone moment. Word about my poetry spread across the campus and I was invited to recite the poem at various events. There I was, using my *blacker-than-me* syndrome to position myself for a fight, yet to my surprise it caused me to be acclaimed, if only for a short moment. I wasn't prepared for that. Could my syndrome cause me to increase instead of decrease? More on this subject later.

To this point, I have spoken about a particular syndrome that plagued my life. How did this revelation come to be? How did I discover the *blacker-than-me* syndrome? When I was discharged from the Navy in 2007, I ended up in a bad place. Prior to getting out of the military, I had a job lined up, but two weeks prior to my discharge, a deliberate action by a navy officer, that was sanctioned the U.S. Navy, put my security clearance into question, resulting in me losing a six-figure job and becoming jobless for six months, with my family and me surviving on the severance pay I received from the U.S. Navy and unemployment benefits.

I have encountered many dark days in my life, but the days leading up to my discharge from the Navy were among the darkest. The details surrounding my military experience could fill a book, so I will spare you the messy details. Eventually I landed a job with Walgreens as an executive assistant manager—sounds cool, huh? I must be honest here, working in retail after fourteen years of military service proved to be the most challenging six years of my professional life. Yet it was during my time at Walgreens that one of my co-workers invited me to attend a meeting about personal development. Thinking it was some type of multi-level marketing business, I reluctantly attended. Expecting some type of business pitch, I was pleasantly surprised when I realized that this was truly a self-help program.

At the end of the session there was an opportunity to sign up for a week-long intensive. Of course, there was a substantial cost associated with this course; however, I didn't hesitate to sign up. Now, I needed to figure out how to pay for it. One thing's for sure: When God has ordained something on your behalf, He always provides access to the resources necessary to bring it to pass, and this was no different. This brings me to another tool I used to help overcome the grip of my *blacker-than-me* syndrome: **faith in God or a higher power.** If God says it is done, it's imperative that you must possess the faith to help activate the movement of God in your life. Not trying to sound preachy, but I have seen enough miracles in my life to know that faith works when it is put to work.

Some of you may have heard of this company before—The Landmark Forum. If you haven't, I suggest you look them up. They can be revolutionary. The place was packed, and I remember having to park quite a way from the building. Each session lasted twelve hours and much of the content was private, so most of what we experienced we could not share with our family or with those who were not part of the program. Out of respect for the creators of the program, I will only share in this book the sessions we were allowed to share with our friends and family, which just so happens to be the session that changed my life forever and led to the writing of this book.

Prior to us leaving for the night, the facilitator asked what I thought was a strange question: "Are you controlled by a seven-year-old?" I found that question to be both intriguing and interesting, and I was looking forward to the next session. Seeing that all of my kids were older than seven, I was wondering how this could be. When the session started, the facilitator began by saying that between the ages of five and nine, we all experience a traumatic event that will affect the outcome of our lives and control the trajectory of what we become in life. I was like, "Wow, that's a trip!" I began to think back over my life and as you have already read, I was seven when I was given the title "blacker-than-me," and when I ruminated on the events of my life up to that point, I discovered that I had spent all of my life trying to *not* be "blacker" than anyone. This desire affected every decision that I ever made, from where I wanted to go to school, what I should study, and what I would eat to what languages I would study and what type of martial art I would practice. I mean *everything* was influenced by this discovery. What a revelation! Although I wish I could take full credit for the discovery of my *blacker-than-me* syndrome, I can't. I personally must give thanks to the Landmark Forum for providing the pathway to discovery. However, I can at least take credit for calling it a syndrome.

That age range (five to nine years old) is key in discovering the origin of many of the syndromes I encounter. When I discuss syndromes with others, nearly 98% of these people can point to an incident that happened to them between the ages of five and nine that has adversely affected them in some way. Those who fall outside that upper range can typically turn to an incident that may have exacerbated their syndrome, and upon further discussion, we tend to land on an incident that does fall within that range. These discussions are not designed to reopen old wounds or unearth horrible memories. Instead, the discussions are aimed at bringing about an explanation as to why certain things occur the way they do. I will forever be grateful to the Landmark Forum.

Transparency moment: I have chosen to utilize the adjective "my" when addressing the *blacker-than-me* syndrome. The term "my" is a possessive word, which gives me control over it. So now, instead of the syndrome having control over me, I can take possession of the syndrome. Now, when I make a significant decision, I can determine if I'm making the choice based on my syndrome or because I want to. This rationale has allowed me to move away from decisions that might have been made because I was trying not to be "blacker than" someone. Imagine the empowerment. Despite feeling empowered from my newfound discovery, the one thing I found difficult to move past was the feeling I had while I was "*Walking While Dark.*"

CHAPTER 8

WALKING WHILE DARK... MY LIFE IN THE SHADOWS

WALKING WHILE DARK

BY COURTNEY LARoY PATTERSON

To walk while dark is
really an untold story.
It lacks the glamor, the
glitz and all life's glory.
Eyes all upon me
trying to figure my path
Assumptions that I am
filled with nothing but wrath
I am called a gangster, a pusher

pimp, abuser, and crook
The kind they see hanging by
his neck over the brook.
Uneducated, dumb, a pure
danger to us all
If I question you loudly
it's the police that you call
I am no monster and
my love flows deep.
Although you mistreat me
my forgiveness I do keep
To emerge from the shadows
and stand in the light.
To be viewed as an equal
now that's well worth my fight
I will beat the stereotypes
until my battle is won.
Lord please remove this curse
from my daughter and my son.
There are days I want
to slowly stroll in a park
But I have to be careful when
walking while dark.

The killing of George Floyd at the hand of four white cops was not only a wake-up call for America, but also the world. For the first time in my life, I witnessed an international outcry for the public killing of a black man. As I watched this unfold on TV, I was filled with mixed emotions. Here I was witnessing a man, a black man, die before my eyes, and his only true sin was that he walked the earth while black. I served in the military for almost fourteen years, and I witnessed my fair share of combat, but this killing was different; I could easily envision myself in George's place. I cringed every time I saw that video play across my TV set, and listening to this grown man call out for his mom in his dying moments pulled at my heart and I think I personally called my mom almost daily.

When the guilty verdict was announced, there was a collective sigh of relief. Justice was finally served…or was it? As I saw and listened to the sentencing of this white police officer, I couldn't help but have a feeling of empathy for this guy. The issue here is that I didn't want to have any level of sympathy towards this now convicted killer. I was angry with myself for having a heart. Was this act germane to me specifically or with the black race in general? After all, we are spiritual and forgiving people. But not this time, please! Let me relish the fact that someone (white) was being punished for committing atrocities against black people.

With the video of Mr. Floyd's daughter saying, "Daddy changed the world!" constantly playing over the airways, I couldn't help but wonder, did he really? Sweetheart, I hope you're right. At the time of this writing, I and the world have witnessed the needless killing of several additional black men, whose only crime, in my humble opinion, was that they were walking while black. I have often wondered if there exists a silent honor between dark-skinned blacks. In my research and in talking with dozens of dark-skinned blacks, I have discovered that many of them, me included, feel alone in their walk. Everyone feels that their suffering is unique to them, and even in the company of other dark-skinned blacks, they find it hard to intermingle because they feel that he or she can't relate to my suffering. Little do we realize that our suffering is more alike than not and that we could probably relate strongly to one another's pain, but because we tend to be isolationist, bridging that gap can be a very daunting task. From my research I can conclude that there is an honor that exists between dark-skinned blacks because there is a common thread woven between us all.

When I walked the streets in my youth, I was never surprised when white people would go out of their way to avoid directly passing me. No, it never feels good, but the act is not earth-shattering. Maybe I looked mean or unapproachable. Maybe what I was giving off triggered a reaction in them. Could I be culpable in some way? Of course. Although my *blacker-than-me* syndrome wants to chip in and start shifting blame, I know it's not my skin tone that precipitated the act. This belief was corroborated by a 2020 article by Keith and Campbell that asserted that whites do not perceive any meaningful differences existing between light and dark-skinned blacks. Yes, history tells us that during slavery, slave owners did show preferential treatment to the lighter slaves, but in keeping with the temperature of the article, whites did see them all as one particular thing: slaves.

When I experience that same reaction from people of my race, the questions that arise are indeed different. Unfortunately, my *blacker-than-me* syndrome goes into full effect. There is little doubt that when facing any type of adversity at the hands of others, my *blacker-than-me* syndrome is the first to chime in, loudly. Yet, a 2019 article by Kaitlyn Greenidge proved to me that my syndrome wasn't too far off. According to Greenidge, some of the stats were astonishing. It was discovered that there exists a difference in pay between dark-skinned and light-skinned men, with dark-skinned men being paid significantly less. There is also agreement that light-skinned blacks are viewed to be more intelligent than their darker counterparts. I could continue with stat after stat, but I think you get the point.

Remember I spoke earlier about how the neighborhood girls were going ape crazy over the bow-legged light skinned brothas in the 1980s? It was in 1982 that the Pulitzer Prize winning novelist Alice Walker coined the phrase *colorism* (Norwood, 2015). According to Norwood, colorism is simply defined as "the prejudicial or preferential treatment of the same race of people based solely on their color." Simply put, the darker you were, the worse you were treated. Let's be honest with one another: colorism did not suddenly show up in the early 80s. There is an abundance of historical evidence that "colorism" was prevalent during slavery, and an argument can be made that this ill treatment of people based on physical appearance dated back to early biblical times. Despite these recorded facts, the colorism in the 80s was in your face, and the girls had no problem reminding you of your "shortcomings." But listen, I had slightly bowed legs; didn't that count for something?

I got married at a pretty young age (more on that later), and despite having a lovely wife, my syndrome was constantly at work: "Oh this was a mercy wedding"; "She's dark skinned as well so you two were made for one another"; "She was probably dealing with her own syndrome and settled for you," and on and on. The truth of the matter is this: Your syndrome does not want to see you happy. Your syndrome constantly wants to keep control of the narrative. Because your syndrome typically stems from a place of weakness, it knows what buttons to push and, more importantly, when to push them. James 4:7 (NKJV) says, *"Therefore submit to God. Resist the devil and he will flee from you."* I will offer this to you: Resist the voice of your syndrome and it will be silenced. But just like the devil, the voices of your syndrome will also return. Keep in mind that the devil, being the father of lies and confusion, heavily influences that voice stemming from your syndrome.

The first major argument I had with my wife came about only a few days after we revealed our marriage to the world (well, at least to our family). Don't worry; I will explain this in the next chapter. We fought over the proper way to make a bed. Did I mention we were young and stupid? Proof positive. I mean, it got heated. All this over catch edge up or down and proper hospital corners? But this was an example of two completely different worlds coming together as one, and the proper making of our bed took center stage. Our next big fight took place a few years later, but this topic of contention was a lot more serious. My wife is a few years older than me and for some reason she could hear her biological clock ticking, even though we both were in our early twenties. She was in the camp that said, "I want children now! Ahora! Pronto!" You get the idea. Naturally, I was in the camp that believed I was too young to have someone calling me dad. The fight ensued and this brought us to the brink where we were reconsidering our life together. Eventually we agreed on a timetable of when we would attempt to build our family.

I had recently joined the Navy and we had relocated to Orlando, Florida, to begin my career. I chalked up this baby notion to her being alone at home while I was at work training. Surely if she got a job, all this baby talk would go away for a while. I was wrong because my wife figured that she could work and be pregnant at the same time, and now more money was coming into the house, so the timing was perfect. Big miscalculation on my part. When the decision was made that we would get pregnant, my wife seemed to get pregnant instantly. I was like, "Man, you didn't play huh?" *Transparency moment*: Although I used my youth as a reason for resisting children, actually I feared transferring that "curse of being a dark-skinned individual in this world" to my kids. My fear was so tangible that I wanted to hold back the one thing that my wife desired… a family. Yes, I was being selfish. I readily admit this.

Watching my wife go through the progressions of pregnancy, I found myself strutting around the house like a peacock. Hours turned into days, days turned into weeks, weeks to months, and months led us, finally, to delivery day. We already knew we were having a boy, so he was already named before he made his entry into this world. My wife was in labor for over thirty hours when the nurses burst into our hospital room at four in the morning with the message, "His heart rate is dangerously dropping, and we need to take him!" I was in a daze, akin to that day when my father woke me to inform me of my Aunt Stevie's death. My wife was now being prepped for an emergency C-section. In just a few moments our son would make his grand entrance into the world. After they prepped her, she was wheeled into the delivery/surgery room.

One thing I didn't know was that my wife would be conscious during the entire procedure. They had me, in my surgical scrubs, on the side of the barrier, sitting next to my wife's head. She and

I made small talk as we both were shielded from what was taking place on the other side of that barrier. After about thirty minutes or so, the surgeon said, "Okay, Mr. Patterson, we are about to deliver your son." With camera in hand, I stood up and peered over this barrier that had once separated me from a completely unexpected scene. As I jumped up, I immediately started snapping pictures before the reality of what I was looking at registered in my mind. Yes, there was our son, all pink and slimy, crying to let the world know he was here, but the other scene stopped me dead in my tracks.

There it was—all my wife's insides were on the table. I even think I saw her heart beating, along with her other vital organs sprawled out on the table. With my mouth wide open I switched between looking at this gaping hole in my wife to looking down at her face and watching her looking around like she was window shopping. I probably switched back and forth between those scenes at least a half dozen times, and before my brain re-engaged with my mouth, I screamed out these words, "C you should be dead, everything you own is on the table!" Sensing my shock, the attending nurse slowly eased me back next to my wife's head.

In the confusion of the moment, I had totally forgotten about CJP1, whom they had whisked away to get cleaned up to be presented to mom and dad. Soon the nurse brought him over to us and just like that, we were a family. I was a dad, and my son didn't appear to be dark like me. Crisis averted! Now, I thought, I can do this dad thing without *that* worry. I could hear the surgeons on the other side of the barrier talking about stuff that had nothing to do with putting my wife back together. I remember yelling over to the other side, "Put everything back in the way you found it!" They laughed, but I was as serious as a heart attack (or maybe I felt I was having one).

An hour later, mommy, baby, and I were resting as a family in our small hospital room. This scenario would play itself out once again four and a half years later when our daughter CJP2 was born. This time I chose not to look at the child behind the curtain. We were now the proud parents of a boy and a girl, and we needed to shut down the factory before we interrupted the perfect balance of the family. As time passed, my deepest fears started to manifest as my children began to darken before my eyes. It felt like every time they woke up, they were one shade darker. I know it's a bit of an exaggeration on my part, but God was microwaving them in their sleep, and there was nothing I could do to stop it. Their shade fell somewhere between my wife's and mine. One thing I told myself was that I would never intentionally draw attention to their skin tone because society would do that for me, and that I was prepared to have that talk if and when it came about; it never did. Today, both my children walk this earth with their heads held high and both are very comfortable in their skin.

As I stated earlier in this book, we all have syndromes, but I can say with all sincerity that neither one of them has suffered their own *blacker-than-me* syndrome. Of course, this society will remind them of their color and send them home to us to pick up the pieces. After their birth, I made it my life's mission to keep a positive approach for my kids with regards to their complexion. I remember when I was a kid, someone very close to me, in a fit of rage, referred to me as a black monkey. I felt so alone and uncovered, and I made a promise I would never make anyone, especially my kids, feel that way. To this day I despise monkeys…guess why? Words do build as well as destroy. Although I positioned myself to shore up my kids when those attacks happened, to my chagrin, the talks never happened. Were they just keeping it to themselves? Were they trying to shield me? The Lord only knows. When I reflect on my kids, my biggest concern lay more with my daughter due to the stigma placed upon dark skinned girls, in connection with her extreme sensitivity. Regardless, there is one characteristic that distinguishes the black woman from any other: her lips.

LIPS OF A BLACK WOMAN... POWER IN THE TONGUE

LIPS OF A BLACK WOMAN

BY COURTNEY LaROY PATTERSON

Thick, shapely, full and
so ready to engage
I love the ruby red image
you placed on that page
When happy they uncover
teeth white as the snow
When pressed against mine
it's affection they show
Soft like cotton and

often touched by the wind
Words pass through them
saying let us begin
Delicious in brown
maroon, or green like moss
Shining like diamonds from
light reflecting off your gloss
Some guys go for legs, thighs
eyes or even hips
But nothing is as sexy
As a black woman's lips.

One of all the things that black women tend to confront on a continuous basis is the sexual objectification by men and the media. I must admit that the poem preceding this chapter seems to follow this pattern. As sexy as I find black women in general, this chapter will focus on the plight of the black woman. I knew it would be a difficult task to write about the black woman's perspective through the pen of a black man. To assist me with capturing the essence of the black woman's voice, I solicited women's thoughts to get me through this chapter, and I hope that I accurately and effectively applied their voice.

This was a well-anticipated chapter, as I get to not only talk about and revel in the power and resilience of black women, but I also get to bring awareness to what black women see as the greatest challenge they face today. You may be wondering: how does my *blacker-than-me* syndrome apply here? In an earlier chapter we touched on how my syndrome affected my relationship with women; in this chapter we will once again visit in detail how black women contributed to my syndrome. In the last chapter I mentioned my concern regarding my daughter being a dark-skinned woman in this society. Although my daughter realized early that she was darker than most of her friends and classmates, she was never made to feel "less than" due to her complexion. As a father who had to deal with that in my youth, I relish the idea that my dark-skinned daughter doesn't have to deal with "that," at least not at the level that I was subjected to. Yet my daughter suffers from her own syndrome that stems from an illness which she suffered in her youth. I soon discovered that syndromes are not inherited or passed down but are instilled within, either consciously or unconsciously. One thing that I unfortunately do realize is that colorism will affect her, and the fact that she's a woman means that the colorism she'll face will be at a level that even I did not experience; society dictates that fact as an accepted norm.

In three separate studies concerning women of color, specifically dark-skinned black women, they are always portrayed as the loud, uncouth, hypersexual Jezebel type. These studies went on to say that in our society, especially in the media, black women are portrayed as sexual targets. Now having a daughter, I found it was my duty as a father to somehow shield her from this reality. But when I think back on my childhood (we are talking about middle school age), I realized that I also objectified women and viewed them as sexual objects to satisfy whatever deranged passions I had. Now tell me, how did a child develop such a warped sense of perception regarding women? Glad you asked. Remember my uncle from earlier in the book, the one I wanted to emulate and follow his every move? Well, he had a stash of Playboy magazines under his mattress, and I can't quite remember how I discovered them, but my first exposure to pornography occurred when I was at the tender age of five or six. Of course, at that age, I didn't know what I was looking at per se; however, I do know I felt a certain way when I looked at these women in those glossy photos. These women were beautiful, and their gestures, positions, and poses looked and felt so inviting that I re-visited them time and time again. I don't believe I encountered any physical reactions while looking at these photos, nor do I feel I was at that time addicted to the feeling. Yet, that exact thing would manifest in my life a tad bit later. My bout with pornography occurred before the advent of my *blacker-than-me* syndrome, but this fascination, which would unfortunately morph into a full-fledged addiction as my syndrome took root, and this addiction would become an instrumental part of my day-to-day existence.

I entitled the poem "Lips of a Black Woman" because I find them the most striking feature of the black woman. Sexy and oftentimes perfectly shaped, the mouth of the black woman intrigued me because of what could come out of it. These lips contained the power to create superheroes, yet at the same time could cut a person down in their prime. With just the curl of her lips, wars could ensue, but her smile could usher in peace. With my *blacker-than-me* syndrome whispering to me that I was *less than*, I feared that the power emanating from those lips would often remind me of what my syndrome was telling me, and unfortunately, they did. While a lot of the words that were tossed my way seemed to be aimed at tearing me down, it was also the lips of a black woman that encouraged me to stand up to a bully and pass the military swimming test—twice! (Side note:

I didn't know how to swim, which speaks to the power of those words.) And it was the lips of a black woman that saved me from attempting suicide. Encouraged me to pursue my advanced college degrees and to write the book that you are currently reading. And even with all that, such encouragement was hard to come by. The words that had the propensity to tear me down mostly came from the tips of a black woman. Since negative comments are known to be 14 to 19 times more powerful than positive ones, such comments would fuel my syndrome and cause it to spread like a cancer.

Transparency moment: I don't know if men are expected to be more okay with women finding them unattractive as opposed to the other way around. But if one of these so-called "unattractive" dudes had what we called "game," he could effectively overcome that deficit. How often have we witnessed some "unattractive" male with a drop-dead gorgeous female? The first thing that typically comes to mind is, "How did he get with that?" From a guy's perspective, the follow-up statement tends to be, "He must have a tight game." What does "game" consist of, honestly? I am sure the answers could vary widely, however, since I am an introvert, my game was nonexistent. I can remember trying to practice my game and sounding like J.J. from the 70s sitcom *Good Times*. Yet, my game always worked with my porno women. I never failed to get them to provide for me the pleasure I was seeking, short-lived though it was.

My obsession with pornography really took off when I was in my middle school years (between the ages of eleven and fourteen). Now magazines no longer had a grip; I had graduated to movies, and with the advent of cable TV, HBO, Showtime, and Cinemax became my virtual porno pushers. Because I didn't have any male role models in my life, outside of my uncles and my mother's male friends that I attempted to get rid of on a routine basis, I only had the men on these shows teaching me how to "treat" women. So, I do not find it surprising that, growing up, I would eventually sexually objectify those females in my life. While I am not proud of my actions, in my immature mind, I thought that's what they wanted; indeed, I was wrong. So, when I started receiving the magnitude of rejections due to my crude actions, I would turn to my "porno" girlfriends to heal my bruised ego. They were so inviting and always smiled at me, and they didn't care about my skin complexion. Whatever I wanted from them they were eager to oblige. For years I was caught in this conundrum, and all my relationships were affected, even the one with my wife. My *blacker-than-me* syndrome was telling me that I was incapable of receiving love and, worse yet, of giving love.

To be honest, this phase was the most difficult to overcome because the pain associated with rejection is still prevalent, and unfortunately, the ability to revisit those porn "girlfriends" has become easier with the introduction of high-speed internet and smartphones. Valuable tools in overcoming the grip of my syndrome with regard to relationships are **communication and honesty**. As my pastor always said, "Confession is good for the soul but bad for your reputation." For me to drown out the voices of my syndrome, it is imperative to have open and honest communications so that collectively, we can devise a plan of action to deal with the pain brought about through rejection by others.

As I mentioned earlier, my syndrome had me convinced that I was not desirable to the opposite sex, but to my surprise, I learned that women, especially dark-skinned women, were experiencing the same level of rejection that I had been subjected to. In an article entitled "Why dark-skinned black girls like me aren't getting married," Dream McClinton chronicles her online dating saga, as she is doubtful about being successful due to her dark skin, suspecting that no one would even pay attention to her profile. The article goes on to provide a disturbing statistic that made me ponder: "55% of light skinned women were married, while only 23% of dark-skinned women had jumped the broom." Goodness, what would be the statistics for men? But I digress.

The article mentions something that I felt resonates with most dark-skinned blacks and is the offspring of my *blacker-than-me* syndrome. That typically we (dark-skinned blacks) feel unwanted except by those who desire to objectify us, causing us to become "empty objects, vehicles for pleasure..."While I feel this is more prevalent among women, the culprit behind this phenomenon is colorism, the ugly stepson of racism. Was colorism the foundation of my syndrome? Arguably, yes. But I sincerely apologize for my role in your objectification. So now I sit here worrying about the possible objectification of my daughter and, to my vexation, she at one point found herself the target of sexual objectification. Oh, how I wish I could shield her, but we all know how the story goes.

When I decided to write this chapter, I wanted to make sure that the voices of the black women could be heard from the pages of this book. I knew that I would write mostly from a guy's perspective, and to help mitigate the bias, I felt it best that you, the reader, heard from black women themselves. To help solidify my thoughts of writing just from a guy's vantagepoint, I posed a single question to both men and women: "What do you think is the biggest challenge facing black women today?" To highlight the contrast of thought between black men and black women, I theorized that men would provide an answer within hours of getting the question, while women would need a lot more time to ponder on their answers. My theory was proven true, as every man I asked this question provided me an answer within six to eight hours after receiving it. Conversely, most of the women I asked responded that they needed at least a couple of days to think about their answer.

Another item I found interesting was the length of the answers given by men versus women. Women's answers were well thought out, passionate, personalized, and lengthy. Men's answers, on the other hand, were the complete opposite. To be honest, I don't think any of the men's answers were formed in complete sentences. To summarize the thought-provoking, lengthy answers offered by the women polled, their answers fell into these categories:

1. the loss of the village
2. feeling insignificant
3. feeling unwanted
4. the "angry black woman" stereotype
5. no black men or lack of quality
6. always need to prove one's worth
7. other black women
8. single motherhood

While this is not an exhaustive list, many of the gripes communicated by black women tended to fall within one or more of the above categories. The list of men's responses is basic:

1. relationships
2. job opportunities

3. equality
4. colorism

Although men in general may never bemoan the plight of the black woman, the men's answers came across as superficial and lacking empathy. To read the complete answers given by the participants of my poll, see the endnote that accompanies this book. Focusing on the list provided by both groups, I discovered that much of what haunts women was almost synonymous with what I was experiencing at the behest of my syndrome. While studying this topic of black women and colorism, I was exposed to some other stereotypes of dark-skinned people that I personally never faced, but stereotypes I heard about dark-skinned blacks were that we were: dirty, unkempt, unintelligent, and sloppy, just to name a few. Wow, all of that just from skin color.

When I was having these frank conversations about colorism and challenges within the black race, particularly with our women, not only did it dawn on me how prevalent syndromes dominate our lives, but also how deeply there is a need to bring awareness to this phenomenon. It also dawned on me that my *blacker-than-me* syndrome stemmed from the bowels of colorism, even before it was a thing, and not necessarily from the channels of a child who had no true animus towards me. All the signs point in this direction. While the young Courtney felt that "Hey, Blacker-than-me" was an insult directed towards him and his character, in reality it was an assault trained upon my shade of black. Now my eyes were wide open.

DARKNESS

SHADES OF BLACK...
THE ACCEPTABLE SHADE AND
WHY

SHADES OF BLACK

BY COURTNEY LaROY PATTERSON

President Lincoln freed the slave in the 1860s through the Emancipation Proclamation

Even though we as a people were freed from the brutal bondage of slavery, the very make-up of our existence in this society has yet to be freed from its impact.

As a casual and somewhat observer in this vast and ever-changing societal structure,

What remains constant would be the four types of African Americans permeating today's society.

It is the nature of man to resist, that of bondage or the thing that impedes mobility or freedom.

Our first type personifies this trait in life and death will be referred to as the **Kunta type**.

Often referred to as militant in nature he is characterized as a non-conformist at best.

He operates within the confines of his ancestral heritage.

He knows his identity and refuses to accept his lot in life as determined by societal standards.

Although personal wealth is not a prevalent in his repertoire,

He understands the need to increase his personal status within this culture.

Not willing to accept the demands and stereotypes placed upon him by the majority race,

He realizes the power and prestige behind the wealth that this society deems so important.

The danger with him lies in his implementation of his philosophies.

He wants to unite with his own kind, but his thoughts are so narrow in utility.

He prays upon his own that do not accept his views.

He is labeled as destructive or a hoodlum.

Education is not important because he feels that the cards are stacked against him anyway.

He is constantly looking up and lacks the desire to change his fate.

His own fear him and separation becomes his ally.

During the time of slavery, not all of the slave owners demonstrated brutality or savage behavior. In recorded history you would see that Thomas Jefferson personified this.

Certain slaves were given the opportunity to learn the craft of reading. Not willing or wanting to accept their position, many of these slaves welcomed the opportunity to learn this much needed craft. I call these the **Douglass type**.

This one understands the importance of education.

He has witnessed how he can be on an even keel with his counterpart, well at least on a knowledge level.

He has discovered that with increased knowledge you can amass increased wealth.

And with increased wealth one can gain almost unlimited power.

With having this power, one soon learns something about the art of influence.

He knows that it isn't necessary to welcome all the beliefs of this society.

He is able to set his filters to only capture the characteristics of this society that benefits him.

He realizes how fortunate he was to have been given the opportunity to elevate and looks to empower others.

He finds out that his enemy is named acceptance and complacency.

He is often mistaken as one of the other types due to his level of education.

Yet he still embraces his heritage and relish within his culture.

Understanding his place in society he strives to influence all of those around him.

His desire to make an impact is unrelenting.

The danger with him is that his desire can become all too consuming.

He soon looks around and discovers that he is alone on his own island.

This next type is commonly mistaken for the Douglass type.

But a closer examination of his motivations, desires and philosophies, it is clear that these two types are worlds apart. Our next type…the **Tom type**.

The house slave was one who was favored by the slave owner.

The slave owners revered him among the other slaves.

His loyalty was evident, and his intentions were well known.

Like the Douglass type, this type was also given the opportunity to learn the craft of reading.

Due to his unmatched loyalty and his acceptance within white society,

He would even "sell out" his own if he thought they would threaten his place in this society.

Although he wore the same dress of color, he never embraced his own nor his culture.

He always looked for an excuse to intermingle, intertwine or interact with mainstream societal ways.

He cannot relate to his own because their ways are no longer his ways.

His desire for acceptance overrides any internal desire to empower those whom he mirrors.

He walks in confusion because of the façade called acceptance from a society that doesn't want him.

Society will use him to their advantage and gain insight into a culture with deep roots.

He is their way in to infiltrate and dilute a race that grows stronger by the numbers.

Once he loses his luster and influence, he is once again thrown back into his own like fish in the sea.

He becomes the proverbial wedge that society desires to lodge between the haves and the have not.

The danger with him is that he uses his own to gain the favor of societal acceptance.

His desire for acceptance causes him to seek outside of his own for love, companionship, self-worth and identity.

He doesn't see the value of his own but tries to distance himself from a label that the same society that he seeks acceptance from has placed upon him.

In all of his efforts he really has no place in society.

He is alone.

Although the next type could arguably be classified as a state of mind, it is listed here as a type because they tend to classify themselves…many times unintentionally. We will simply refer to them as **Victor (victim) types**.

This type can emerge from any of the aforementioned types.

His brashness seems to increase with the lack of education.

He is still in search of his 40 acres and a mule.

He feels that he should be compensated for what his forefathers had to endure during slavery.

"You owe it to me!" is his rally cry.

Despite his wayward approach, he manages to conjure up a following.

He wallows in the pity of others.

Self-pity is his strongest characteristic and ownership is a forgotten word.

Responsibility is only used when it suits him.

In his mind his demise was handed to him by a hateful society.

Self-sufficiency is successfully being accepted within subsidized programs.

Nothing is self-gained, everything shall be handed over to them

Religion becomes their crutch.

Everything is dangerous about this type because the world seemingly is his.

Although they identify more with the Kunta types, their affiliations with the other types are well known.

Victor types come from all walks of life, but once they arrive they all look, act, respond and believe the same.

Victors are cancerous and can infiltrate the tightest of communities.

They don't discriminate yet they are very selective in their fights.

In their minds they have "mastered" the system.

The same system designed to keep them as a Victor type.

The have mastered loss.

Sadly enough, within this society you will encounter all of these types of people.

We may marry some and give birth to others.

Upon close examination of one's character we'll be able to see traces of each type in all of us.

Some types will prove to be more dominant than the others.

But is there a desired type to manifest within your life?

Why does it appear that we are Kuntas when around Kuntas, Douglass around Douglass, Toms around Toms, and Victors around Victors?

Has this society created a more versatile type, once that can relate to all?

If so, we shall name this type **The Chameleon**.

It seems that since the age of seven, I have spent a great deal of my life battling my *blacker-than-me* syndrome. Mind you, most of this battling was done unknowingly, as I wasn't made aware that I even possessed a syndrome until my mid-40s. When I look back over my life, until that moment of discovery, that was an unconscious fight. What exactly constitutes my *blacker-than-me* syndrome? I am glad you finally asked. My *blacker-than-me* syndrome caused me to commit to actions that were essentially aimed at making me *appear* to be *not* blacker than the other blacks in my circle at any moment in my life. Sounds crazy right? Especially when you see me in person, it's pretty difficult to imagine me not being the blackest or darkest person present. I can remember as a child looking at group photos and comparing my skin complexion with those in the picture. Oftentimes wondering to myself if others paid attention to this as well. Although I don't spend a great deal of time making those comparisons today, from time to time I find my eyes darting from people to people in a crowded room or in a group photo, seeing if I out shadowed them and by how much. Why did I place so much energy into this? Simply because I convinced myself that others were doing it as well. Kind of a backhanded exercise of self-centeredness, I suppose. Now you are probably wondering how a dark-skinned man fixates himself to not be darker than the next black person. If you're not, well you should, because I'm going to tell you anyway.

Understand this: I am not so disillusioned that in my twisted mind I meditate in such a way that I somehow become lighter in skin tone than the next man (or woman for that matter). However, the actions and decisions I made throughout my life to this day are pretty darn close to that crazy meditation thing. Referring to the poem preceding this chapter, hopefully it did not take long to determine that when I talk about shades of blacks, I am really referring to types of blacks. I feel confident in believing that most can relate in dealing with various types of blacks highlighted in the poem. Unfortunately, some stereotypes do take a stronghold, but I will make every attempt to not dwell upon them. So, for me to not be blacker than someone, I felt I had to morph into one of the shades of blacks that I felt the situation called for. How did I pull this feat off? The easiest way for me to do this was to place myself in situations where I would be the only black or one among the few.

Growing up in the ghetto of Wellston, Missouri, being the sole black was nearly impossible. My first opportunity came to fruition when I began high school. Thanks to the desegregation program that was beginning in St. Louis, I was offered the chance to attend one of St. Louis County's premier high schools. Mehlville Senior High School had just entered the program at the same time I began high school, and I ended up being one of the participants in St. Louis' new bussing program. To be honest, Mehlville wasn't even on my scan. I wanted to attend Ladue High School for many of the same reasons (good education, lack of black bodies), but the main reason was because I was so in love with my cousin Yvonne, and she attended Ladue, and I loved being in her company. Transparency moment: Yvonne was beautiful, and when she came to visit us in Wellston, all the boys in the neighborhood went nuts. So, to have someone like her paying attention solely to me made me feel loved and special. The fact that she didn't see my color was a first for me. When Yvonne and I were outside, I would stay under her and take pride watching the neighborhood boys turn green with envy. Now that I think about it, she was probably why they wanted to always fight me. Okay Yvonne, I blame you for my childhood battles; nah, you know better. I love you to the moon and back (but once again, I digress).

Regarding the various shades of blackness, I can say attending a predominantly white high school in Mehlville shifted my focus from concentrating so much on my complexion and more towards the shade of my blackness I would adopt. I would quickly learn that a byproduct of my *blacker-than-me* syndrome was to operate within shades or attributes to not seem blacker than the other blacks who were also bussed out to this county school. Another thing I noticed was that in dealing with the white race, colorism is not such a big deal so long as you are portraying the correct shade of blackness in their eyes. I must admit that there were times, at the end of the day, I felt so remorseful because the shade I had to put on that day grieved my spirit-man, not because I was operating openly in sin, but mainly because I was not being my authentic self and I felt like I was living a lie. Who would have thought that being a chameleon could be so exhausting.

I prided myself on always being a bright student, but after I made that decision to use education to make up for what I thought were my faults, I truly became obsessed with education serving as a shield to my color. I can readily admit that the obsession remains to this day. Being a student at Mehlville Senior High would challenge me scholastically, essentially for my entire high school tenure. I had come from the inner-city schooling system, and preparation for high school had not necessarily been a focus of my elementary school. Not only did I find myself in classes I had never heard of before (for example, molecular biology), but also, for the first time ever in my life, I would see grades south of Bs (and on a few occasions, south of Cs). Now the one thing that had served me well to this point in my life was being challenged in a way I had never expected, and I had a decision to make: stay and fight or turn and run back to the confines of my ghetto community, where I knew I could flourish. I decided to stay and fight—and it was a fight.

There had been an earlier moment in my life where my obsession with education almost led to a physical altercation with a fellow student. Being a new student in my third-grade class, I found myself in the midst of a math contest with my classmates. The teacher would stand us in a line and bounce a ball to us, and on this ball were various multiplication problems that we were expected to answer in a specific timeframe before bouncing the ball back to the teacher. If you answered incorrectly or took too long, you were out of line and had to return to your desk. One by one, the students fell and soon there stood only two, me and E, the school bully. Unfortunately, Es' status in the school was unbeknownst to me at that time, so to me he was an impediment to my victory and not a personal physical threat. Oh, poor soul that I was.

E and I battled one another for several minutes, and I could feel his frustration and I reveled in that. In about the fifth round E began ordering me to miss. Who was he to tell me to lose? So, I dug in. Big mistake. Eventually the teacher declared it a draw and both of us were winners. Before I had time to gloat about my victory, E walked over to me and said, "I'm getting you at recess." I was dumbfounded. "Why?" I said to myself. Little did I know that E was not only the school's bully, but he was also the reigning champion in this multiplication contest, and I had bested him. Soon the school bell rang, and I headed outside to meet my fate.

In a typical bully move, E had recruited his little henchmen to fight his battle. E chose M to fight me. Fortunately for me, I was tall for my age, so I welcomed the altercation with M, who I had several inches and at least 20 pounds on. Good thing for me, M realized that as well and refused to fight me. Although the story does not end there, I can honestly say that I never envisioned being smart could lead to an actual physical encounter. While no such altercation would present itself during my time at Mehlville, being the only black in most of my classes proved to be a different type of challenge. As a matter of fact, in both my personal and professional capacity, I have often found myself in situations where I was the only black student present. As a result of me attending a predominantly white school, this soon became a must in all my actions and/or decisions I would make for much of my adult life: I had to be the only one. I began to personally seek out activities that very few, if any, blacks participated in. In my effort to not be blacker than someone, I was willing to deal with the sting and vitriol that accompanied racism and discrimination. I much preferred to focus on being the right shade of my blackness than to deal with the color I was born with. I felt I had power to control the shades, but at what cost?

Although I would never fully "fit in" with the other races of the world, the mastery of my shades allowed me to safely operate within the confines of their world. However, I found myself alienating myself from those within my own race. Because I had spent so much of my life in situations void of many blacks, when I found myself in the company of my own race, I found it difficult to relate. I remember having a conversation and somebody commented, "You sound white." And for a fleeing moment, I relished that. I had made it! I finally was no longer blacker than them. Seriously?!

My syndrome really had me functioning in an alternate world. This bizarre world was my reality. Not because I was trapped in fantasyland; I simply didn't know any better. If it were not for the Landmark Forum, only the Lord knows where I would be in my walk today. Now I am not suggesting you or anyone go and spend money on an intensive like Landmark. Although it worked for me, it may or may not work for you. Of all the tools needed to lessen the grip of your syndrome, **awareness** is but the biggest and, in many ways, the most important. Throughout this book I've given you some tools to utilize post discovery of your syndrome. But if you focus on those years between the ages of five to nine, this is where you are likely to discover the origin of your own.

Let me give you a few final things to contemplate. Even in the throes of your syndrome, sometimes the decisions that may emerge may not adversely affect you. For me specifically, my desire not to be blacker than someone encouraged me to attend events, join organizations or participate in programs that I ordinarily would not have even considered. My fear of failing to achieve the status of not being blacker than others galvanized my resolve to become successful in those endeavors where there was a noticeable lack of black representation, and through my syndrome I felt I had to show the other races that no matter the shade I selected, coupled with uncanny resolve, I would remain on par with them.

When I look back through the lens of my syndrome, focusing upon my shades was very prevalent to my existence in this world. I acknowledge that until Landmark, most of my actions were unconsciously performed because of my lack of awareness. Soon after my awakening at Landmark, my awareness was heightened and now, I possess the power to take a step back and assess my actions and pending decisions though the filter of this question: "Am I doing this because of my syndrome or because I really want to?" Although, my *blacker-than-me* syndrome caused me to participate in things when under normal circumstances I probably would not have given them a second look. I can truthfully say that since I became aware of my syndrome, in conjunction with the tools I laid out in this book, I possessed the power to decide if I would move forward or not.

Is any of this foolproof? Of course not. Just like with an addiction, you never really overcome it, should the right trigger present itself and cause a relapse. The same can be said about personal syndromes. We all make thousands of decisions daily, both consciously and unconsciously, and it is imperative that some of these are scrutinized to determine if they are syndrome-driven or not. I cannot stress enough how crucial awareness is to your success, despite your syndrome. If you need a reminder on how I made my discovery, go back a couple chapters, and reread my Landmark Forum experience. While I would never try to duplicate the life changing exercises by the Landmark Forum, I certainly do hope that this book will incite a Landmark moment in your life.

Prior to becoming aware of my syndrome, being that chameleon was my superpower. Now, for the first time in my life, I have the power to overpower and overcome the grip of my syndrome, and I have succeeded despite it. I am empowered knowing that I have a syndrome and not the other way around. This same empowerment can be gained by you once the steps towards awakening are taken. I look forward to hearing about your change and I celebrate your awareness and eventual overcoming.

CONCLUSION

Everyone deals with some type of syndrome in his or her life. I know that such a statement may appear presumptuous, yet once our syndrome is discovered and identified, we will find that its tentacles are intricately woven within every facet of our lives. In the traditional sense, syndromes are commonly associated with diseases or disorders. It is not ordained that our personal syndromes have to constantly present themselves as negatives throughout our lives. Unlike addictions, syndromes typically are not something that one easily overcomes.

We must realize that most of our reactions and decisions that we face on a daily basis probably stem from an area within our syndromes. Please note, just because I may be diagnosing you with a syndrome does not necessarily equate to you possessing a known ailment or a disease. However, the manifestation of one's personal syndrome can oftentimes be initiated through the actions of others, whether direct or indirect. The traumatic acts aimed at another can easily be the genesis of a syndrome. Such actions can indeed be physical but can also come in the form of the spoken word, yet the results can be equally devastating, or in some instances, worse.

Personal syndromes tend to originate from an area of one's youth, typically between the ages of five and nine. While traumatic actions are typically the genesis of one's syndrome, it is the words coming from the mouths of adult figures or from those who you admire and respect that can have long-lasting, damaging results, contributing to the advancing of the metastasis of one's syndrome. Whether we are aware or not, our syndromes play pivotal roles in the decisions we make daily, be it conscious or not.

Oftentimes, emotional reactions such as anger, despair, or a melancholy disposition are byproducts of our syndromes, and while these emotions can have negative results, these results do not have to become roadblocks or impediments towards successfully navigating the fog of our syndromes. Sometimes our dreams can provide key insights into the purpose of our syndromes if we pay attention and take note. As noted throughout the Bible, God frequently used dreams to get messages into the earth, and from the Bible we see that it is not sinful to question God regarding His actions. Such dialogue between us and our Heavenly Father may provide long-sought answers to what is God's will for our lives and how this may be reflected in our syndromes.

Unfortunately, we live in a society where the color of the skin you wear determines where you fall in the pecking order of things, and without effective coping mechanisms put in place, the effects of this reality can further ostracize and prove damaging. This can come in the form of simply walking the streets or driving the wrong car in the wrong neighborhoods. In dealing with my *blacker-than-me* syndrome, I've found that wearing the wrong shade of skin tone can have a variety of influences upon the actions of the people I may encounter, including law enforcement. Despite my best efforts to not be blacker than those around me, there are constant societal reminders out there that always reminds me that I am, and it does nothing but exacerbate my personal syndrome. The lack of coping structures can also show up in the form of the relationships we may forge. We may ultimately engage with people that are not only bad for us but will also promote our syndromes.

What we have discovered is that we may attract certain people based on our syndrome and not necessarily based on compatibility. We have to take note that our syndromes have made each one of us into who we have become to this day. The characteristics that are formed due to our syndromes are entrenched and cannot be easily rooted out. It is imperative that we do not allow ourselves to be defined by the characteristics of our syndromes. As was discussed earlier in this book, most internal conflicts are aimed at preventing us from obtaining or doing something. Conversely, our syndromes are trying to get us to do something. What we decide to do can determine failure or success. Our spiritual enemy, commonly referred to as the devil or Satan, has a plan to get us to default on our assignment from God, and he uses whatever device or scheme to accomplish that feat, and of course our syndromes are but one of the many that he uses. But we know that God can turn anything around for His glory, and this includes our syndromes.

I liken personal syndromes to bad coaching. Even though all the signs may point to epic failure or defeat, the individual or the team can achieve great success despite bad teaching because of a desire to win which is contained within them. The same can be said about our syndromes; the signs may seem to point towards mediocrity or failure, but because of what God has instilled within all of us, we can have untold success in spite of our deeply rooted syndromes. The syndrome will always remain with us, but once we are aware of its existence and its desire for our lives, we regain the power to forever minimize its overall effect, essentially turning a projected loss into a well-calculated win.

AFTERWORD

Inside My Darkness has been in the works for nearly thirty years. What began as a series of poems, the collection was initially titled *Inside the Darkness* as a play on my skin complexion and the world I was currently living within. It was truly aimed at giving the reader a glimpse of what it was to walk this earth in my skin tone. Of course, it was simply from my vantage point, but in talking with other dark-skinned blacks, I soon discovered that we all shared similar experiences and they could relate to my poems. In some weird and crazy way, I had self-ordained myself as the dark person's spokesperson. But that was short-lived once I entered military service.

Although what happened to me during my fourteen years in the U.S. Navy can be attributed to my skin color, I can say without a doubt that the darkness of my skin tone was secondary, even though I personally felt it played a role when you consider some of the stereotypes that were levied against me upon my exit from service. As a result, my voice for the dark-skinned black was replaced with the voice for the mistreated military black and believe me, that story shall be told. Later, that advocate voice would once again be replaced with self-loathing and self-pity, and I reasoned that the world would never hear this voice again, at least for now. Man was I wrong because God said speak. But what was I going to say, Lord, when I feel no one stands as my ally?

Shortly after my unexpected departure from the military, I met a pastor by the name of Dr. Myles Munroe. I had no idea who he was, but he was the keynote speaker at a Pre-Paid Legal conference I was attending in Atlanta, Georgia. After he finished his message, Dr Munroe decided to lay hands upon someone at the conference and pray for them. Among the hundreds who were in attendance, he focused on me. When he beckoned me to the front of the conference room, I slowly and reluctantly edged myself towards the front of the room. After laying hands upon me and praying for me, he sat down in front of me and began talking to me. While the room was buzzing about, this general in the faith took several minutes out of his life to pour into the life of me, a complete stranger. A moment I will never forget.

When Pastor Myles Munroe went on to his heavenly reward, the words he spoke to me on that day came to life within me. Fast forward to today: His words has served as a catalyst for many of my professional endeavors including the book you are now reading. The perfect follow up to *Inside My Darkness* is to chronicle various interviews and discussions with some successful and no-so-successful dark-skinned blacks. The purpose is aimed at seeing if any of them felt their color affected their plight in life. Outlining the various tools they used to overcome their syndrome can prove invaluable. Stay tuned.

APPENDIX

In an effort to bring a true and accurate account of black women perspectives, I posed this simple yet loaded question to a panel of women and to a group of men. I have to admit that I was stunned at the level and depth of the answers I received.

The question posed was: *What do you feel is the greatest challenge facing black women?*

Before you read the answers, try formulating your own answer and then see if yours align with the participants of this simple yet important poll.

Answers:

Men answer:

"Interesting question because there are different challenges overall based on:

1. Generation
2. Skin Tone
3. Racial Perceptions.

1. Promotion
2. Relationships"

"Me time and financial solvency"

"Only 3 out of 10 black women will marry. Although they are the most educated and upwardly mobile people in the workforce"

Women answer:

"Ok I have given this some thought. There are many challenges facing black women today but the greatest is us not being seen, heard, valued and protected for what we are. Everything has come from us yet we are overlooked, cast aside and unprotected. We deserve better."

"The biggest challenge facing black women today is the lack of protection and care from our men. Back in the day…way in the day, black men looked out for all black women in the community. Now, if a man is not physically in the black woman's home, she is left to protect and defend her own. None of the men in a lot of families consider us enough to make sure we're straight. And if we ask someone outside of the home to help, it's like we're a bother, which discourages us from asking. We have to make our own repairs, move our own houses, secure our own homes, etc. It makes us feel unwanted or insignificant."

"Emotionally suppressed. We all know the angry black woman stereotype. With that stereotype, you can't just be angry when any other person would be in your situation. You try to suppress your perfectly normal feelings in fear of being labeled an angry black woman. That's not healthy at all. The angry black woman stereotype is often used against us in passive aggressive ways.

People will purposely anger us. Then when we react, they play victim. 9 times out if 10, we are seen as the aggressor.

I have a list of issues but this one is very personal to me. Constantly having to prove myself as being educated, a Christian, non drinker, non smoker, never using drugs, non partier, serious, intelligent, non criminal, hard working and sexually abstinent."

"The village is gone doing a lot on your own struggling when you don't have to.. family loosing their roots"

"Everyone is out for self no one is helping each other anymore. Stop down talking about others that isn't doing as well and besides that if you see or know that someone is going through something help them out and if you can't help ask them what it is that I can do for you"

"Some black women can't be themselves publicly. Can't wear bright colored hair, long Nails, weave, can't have a good time without us being perceived as ghetto. The biggest challenge being black is simply that. We go to the hospital to conceive a place we think is supposed to be safe they silence our rights and force us into c sections. It's like we have to be strong because just like the black culture without gender attached we have to be because the system wants us to fail it's a rigged system where they want us to work our butts off have kids (but don't have too many Cus if we get government assistance now we robbing them and "mooching" off them for resources" when we can barely afford to live on our own and support our offspring . The biggest challenge is that we don't have a village like the others said. We need each other. But because of how we were raised by our ancestors some of us look at other black women and judge them instead of talking to them or learning from a sister. I could go on forever but that's just off the top of my head"

"Being the most educated demographic in the United States now, we have to balance being the breadwinner, wife, a mother and mental health"

"There are many challenges facing the Black woman today. None of these challenges affects every Black woman the same, nor are all challenges faced by Black women, the same challenge for every Black woman. One of the biggest challenges for Black women today is, unfortunately, the Black woman."

"Today, there are some Black women who are more concerned with elevating themselves. They will use other Black women as a stepping stool to rise above them. Instead of elevating, uplifting, or supporting each other, they use others' weaknesses to their advantage to rise above them. They are degrading other Black women, so they can appear to be better. Back in the day, Black women helped each other. The village was strong. If one struggled, the others would help out. I'm not saying this isn't still going on today. I'm just saying you don't see it as often. In some communities, Black women gather and talk about each other. They have too much free time to tear each other down, but no time to help build each other up. The village is no longer working together as one. Instead, they are working against each other, fighting to be seen as number one. Like others have said in this thread, I could go on and on with other examples. If I did, you will eventually begin to see the pattern. Regardless of educational level, living environment, or occupational field, you will notice a common denominator, the Black woman. I am a proud Black woman and my opinion is not intended to tear down any other

Black woman. My opinion is merely my observation of some of the Black women I have come across in my lifetime, so far."

"The biggest challenge facing black women today is unknowingly, being the demise of the black community by repeating the cycle of having children out of wedlock with often, young unemployed, uneducated boyfriends without a plan for their own future nor for the child's future."

"Biggest challenge in business, work:

I think gaining respect of the opposite sex for sure, especially in a company where men are the majority

Life in general:

A fact that many (most) black women are single parents, so bringing up a child, especially in these modern times, truly a real challenge with so many influences from outside. Very hard to stand your ground and doing the right thing, while being firm and fair"

"Well I'm not in the business world so I can't elaborate on that, but I am a black woman. I think the biggest challenge is from the time you step into anything is that as a black woman you almost feel obligated to prove yourself because people judge you from the jump and we start to doubt in our abilities to reach success and goals in our lives. We always think that we must always be strong and that is not true we may be soft also, we are human. I'm brave enough to say that we as black women are our own biggest challenge, because we don't support and motivate each other as we should. Black women often compete against each other while together we are way stronger."

"A black woman's biggest challenge is feeling or believing that one needs to be extraordinary to do the ordinary. Causing many to go over the top to prove oneself, so much so that they loose themselves. The detailed journey to success has been lost as the colors changed. Our secrets have been breached, therefor no one is sharing anything anymore, Lack of trust, black eat black, we become ruthless, territorial. We can't work in unity. Because we haven't seen it in our culture. We don't understand that we each have a piece of the puzzle. We have been strategically separated in shades of black to cause of to lose the root of truth.

That we are stronger together."

"I think the biggest challenge is believing in yourself. Many of us give up too soon.

Our ideas are different and support takes time to build....so the beginning is rough.

I also believe finding the right mentors are essential to our success. Within the black community you don't find many mentors who are willing to share their journey with up and coming business owners."

"Not seeing our self worth. Handling l/acting/thinking from the prospective of a minority. Yes we have to go the extra mile but we play the victim role too often. Stand your ground. Be the woman you know you are from the inside out.

Portraying confidence makes a lot of difference in how people receive you."

"Being Single but having a strong desire to be married and have children but facing the fact that the clock is ticking and we are close to hitting the danger zone for having children"

"1st one: Being a Woman in a Men's world is already a major issue. 2. Being Black in this GALAXY is seen as a Curse / lowest of all the RACES. So, combining both is 1 of the hardest challenge We/Black Women face. We have to prove ourselves not only to other races and genders but to our Black Men that we are STRONG & EQUIPED QUEENS. We have to work 10 to 20x harder than other races and genders and that's not fair to us."

"Being strong, but not too strong at the same time. Black women have always been considered as strong. We have been expected to take care of everybody from spouses, friends, children, and ourselves. We take care of everything and consider everyone. Throughout history, we have taken care of other races (slavery – we took care of the slave masters, their wives, and children). We have been seen as the strong ones during adversity. We are expected to be strong and carry our families when men have been absent. With that being said, when we are seen as smart, educated, or powerful, we are looked upon as arrogant or too strong. When we are seen as too strong, our Black men don't want to deal with us because we have attitudes. We get traded for white women who are passive or submissive. So, the biggest challenge for Black women is finding the right balance to fit in and still be accepted for who we are without being labeled."

"Ohh btw i totally forgot I had an answer for u on your Q., I think respect towards women owning their own is lacking or seems a treat to certain people"

ENDNOTES

Berohn, K. & Cruz, A. (2021, May 5) A dream expert explains why you're dreaming about death. The Cut. Retrieved from www.thecut.com/article/dreams-about-death.html

Boyd, J. (2016, December 5). Tears and black masculinity. Abernathy. Retrieved from https://abernathymagazine.com/black-men-cry.

Hannon, L. et al. (2020, November 2). Do white people see variation in black skin tones? Reexamining a purported outgroup homogeneity effect. Social Psychology Quarterly. 84(1), Retrieved from https://doi.org/10.1177/0190272520961408

Jacobs, T. (2018, September 11). Research suggests black women are more likely to be objectified and dehumanized: Serena Williams is not alone in having grounds to suspect bias. Social Justice. Retrieved from https://psmag.com/social-justice/black-women-are-more-likely-to-be-objectified-and-dehumanized

McClinton, D. (2019 April 8). Why dark-skinned black girls like me aren't getting married. The Guardian. Retrieved from https://amp.theguardian.com/lifeandstyle/2019/apr/08/dark-skinned-black-

Norwood, K. J. (2015). If you is white, you's alright. . . ." Stories about colorism in America, 14 WASH. U. GLOBAL STUD. L. REV. 585 (2015), https://openscholarship.wustl.edu/law_globalstudies/vol14/iss4/8

Liquids & Solids Spirit. (n.d.) Dream in black and white? (8 spiritual meanings). Retrieved from https://www.liquidsandsolids.com/dream-in-black-and-white/

Marketinguae. (2020, September 20) What's the difference between a syndrome and a disorder? Igenomix. Retrieved from https://www.igenomix.net/blog/what-is-the-difference-between-a-syndrome-and-a-disorder/

Matthews, A. D. (2018, Winter). Hyper-sexualization of black women in the media. Gender & Sexuality Studies Student Work Collection, 22. Retrieved from https://digitalcommons.tacoma.uw.edu/gender_studies/22

Samuels, A. (2010, January 11) The ugly roots of the light skin/dark skin divide. Newsweek. Retrieved from https://www.newsweek.com/ugly-roots-light-skindark-skin-divide-213518

Stanton, A. G. et al. (2022, June). Black women's experiences of gendered racial sexual objectification, body image, and depressive symptoms. Science Direct. *41*. Retrieved from https://doi.org/10.1016/j.bodyim.2022.04.914

"What exactly are syndromes?" (2017, December 07). Retrieved from https://healthcare.utah.edu/the-/scope/list/2011/12/what-exactly-are-syndromes

All biblical scriptures used in this book were taken from the New King James Version.

www.ingramcontent.com/pod-product-compliance
Lightning Source LLC
Chambersburg PA
CBHW060437090426
42733CB00011B/2303